think

About Jim Greenwood

'I didn't feel I'd started coaching until I'd read Jim Greenwood.'
Ian McGeechan OBE, British Lions coach

'Jim Greenwood's books are my inspiration; they are my "bible".'
Bill Freeman, as Director of Coaching, NZ Rugby Football Union

'You know this man as Mr Rugby, but I saw him play. . .'
Dr Gerrit Pool, Stellenbosch and Western Province, introducing Jim Greenwood
to a student

Jim Greenwood was a distinguished player – captain of Scotland, British
Lion, Barbarian – before becoming a highly influential coach. Supported
by his worldwide coaching-method tours, his two books, *Think Rugby*
and *Total Rugby*, have had a major impact on the development of the
game. In recognition of this, the National Coaching Foundation have
recently awarded him the prestigious Geoffrey Dyson trophy and elected
him – the only rugby coach – to the inaugural Coaching Hall of Fame.

Also available by Jim Greenwood:

Total Rugby
Fifteen-man Rugby for Coach and Player
Fourth Edition

'In the new age of professionalism with its emphasis on
entertainment, *Total Rugby* is more pertinent than ever before.'
Don Rutherford, as Director of Rugby, RFU

Also available from A & C Black:

The RFU Guide to Fitness for Rugby
Rex Hazeldine and Tom McNab

The RFU Handbook of Safe Rugby

The RFU Rugby Union Referee's Manual
Richard Greensted

So the generalised system reads like this:

- we need *models*, based on principles, to clarify as many aspects of play as possible;
- we need *feedback* to indicate whether the player (or the opposing team) has departed from the model;
- we need to register and refine the knowledge we gain from feedback so it is available to us as *expectations* or what's likely to be significant and the best way of dealing with it;
- if we need to *scan* our expectations, we do it in order of likelihood; and
- *our choice of action*, implicit in our expectation, has been established in practice.

You'll see that this is less a method of discovering new knowledge – though the need to refine our expectations is a constant incentive to that – than of organising what we already know into an immediately available form. It enables us to act quickly and decisively, the usual requirement not only for coaching but for refereeing, selecting, writing about the game and, above all, playing. The odds are that you've read the foregoing with a specific interest: because you're a coach, you read it in terms of coaching. Go back now, and read it in terms of those other activities.

It works. After I opened a course in Boston, Mass., with a lecture on the general method:

- Fred Howard, the excellent international panel referee, came up to say how much it had clarified his consciousness of how he worked;
- Les Cusworth, an equally accomplished tactical decision-maker (though not always given a chance to show it at international level) agreed; and
- Alan Davies, whose coaching had done so much to restore Welsh international rugby, had just written an article recommending it to coaches.

I'm moderately sure, too, that other, less noted rugby people use something like this approach without being conscious of doing so: the hope is that once they recognise it, they can apply it more effectively.

Let's now look at how it works in some interested groups.

THE PLAYER: *the stand-off as tactical decision-maker*

He's watching a situation develop towards a tactical point – a ruck, say, 20m from the right touch, just outside the opposing 22m line:

- he has a clear mental model of what the opposing defence will look like;

- he has clear expectations of where it's likely to be weak – for example wide on the left; down the blind-side; under the posts;
- his first expectation is right: their right wing is close in;
- he and his team-mates know precisely how his team can get the ball wide fast – he calls it, and off they go.

THE SELECTOR: *assessing a flanker*

He's watching a maul at which the player he's assessing is defending at the back on the right:

- he has a clear mental model of the player's role – he's found out from the coach what it is: to get wide and drive forward on the first opposing player;
- he expects the player not to get wide enough, and not to commit himself to going forward fast enough;
- he does get wide; he does go forward fast enough . . . good;
- he checks it off, and concentrates on the next situation in the job specification, knowing that he'd better check again late in the game to see whether fatigue affects performance, but that he can compliment the player at least in that respect at the end of the game. He should also liaise with the coach on points that need attention in the flanker's play.

THE REFEREE: *refereeing a line-out*

- He has a clear mental model of what the legal line-out should look like – any gross difference needs inspection;
- he has clear expectations of what this particular team are likely to do: pressurise by stepping as a line on to the line of touch, so that they're in the strongest position to control the ball, to exert pressure on the opposing jumpers, to get in behind the ball;
- he fixes his attention on the exact line of touch midway down the line-out: they are pressurising;
- he blows up and awards a penalty, explaining why to the offending captain and assuring him that he'll notice it next time as well.

THE REPORTER: *watching a cup final on behalf of a quality paper*

- He has a clear model of the relative strengths of the two teams;
- he expects certain aspects of play to be critical: Team A's ability to keep possession at the breakdowns; Team B's domination of the line-out;

- whatever else he sees, he checks out both, keeping a score on each aspect;
- he writes a report with very hard statistical fact to back up his opinions. Whether his expectations are right or wrong, he has news!

In all of these cases it is evident that the observer is concentrating on particular aspects of play. This goes back to two previous assertions:

IF YOU DON'T LOOK FOR IT, YOU WON'T SEE IT
IF YOU TRY TO SEE EVERYTHING AT ONCE,
YOU'LL END UP SEEING NOTHING

Of course, your attention to particular aspects won't monopolise your attention: you'll register the unexpected at the same time. And you're involved in a continuing process which lets you shift your focus progressively.

So how do we cultivate this process?

STEP ONE: ADOPT A MODEL

The strength of the original method lay in having a mechanical model of the technique and a way of checking it out systematically. It had two practical functions.

1. It helped us take beginners (for example, accomplished back row forwards who would benefit from acquiring an effective scrum-half pass) and give them a quick, concise, accurate and understandable model for consistent performance.
2. It gave us a very accurate, systematic way of spotting faults, and then of correcting them.

The model in question was biomechanical – typically, a model of throwing adapted to the demands of rugby. It has been tested out and established. It has much of the validity of an exact science. It's doubtful if we can equal this degree of validity in other kinds of model. But can we use models at all? I believe, as I've said, that we can, and that many of us do.

We can create a model of any aspect of play of which we understand the underlying principles. If we understand the principles of counter-attack, for example, we can design an effective model of how our team is going to counter-attack, give clear criteria of where and when it's on, and spot weaknesses in execution. As always, this is best done as a joint operation between coach and players. We can then apply it exactly as we applied the biomechanical model to technical performance, but it must remain open to amendment, refinement, development, and possible restructuring. It simply represents our best understanding now.

Reaching these principles is hard work, but the effort is justified because it accelerates the players' judgement. In effect, it allows them to apply the observation system for themselves.

THE FULLBACK: *on his 10m line, centrefield, under a misdirected relieving kick. Should he/how should he counter-attack?*

- He has a clear mental *model* of what the opposing defence should look like: front three coming up in line; fullback deep behind them; forwards spreading across before coming up; he has a clear mental *model* of what he himself needs: space to go forward, immediate support, and a margin of safe space behind him;

- he *expects* (with this particular opposition) that the front three won't be in line, and won't be on top of him, and that he will have support, because the team have practised it; he expects to run;

- but his immediate feedback shows opposing front three organised and close;

- immediately he uses a fall-back plan, kicks deep to the fullback's left and chases after it.

How do we uncover principles and devise models? You may be able to apply the *first method* in searching for answers – it depends on the complexity of the question. If you're concerned with simple, discrete facts, such as effective binding with the opposing prop for your loose-head, then yes, the method will be easy enough to apply. You look for *what* international loose-heads are doing, and you think about it, and discuss it, until you grasp the principles behind it – the *why*. You look at how opposing tightheads react, to give you a line on the effectiveness of different methods. You check out collapses on the loose-head side. In other words, you focus intently on a single position till you've a grasp of good form, and from it deduce the principle. The principle is important, because your loose-head may not have the physical advantages of his international counterparts, and may not be able to apply their methods. But if he grasps the purpose, he may be able to adapt the methods adequately.

On the other hand, if you're concerned about a fairly complex issue, it may be difficult for you to establish what's going on, or to distinguish it from what's meant to be going on but is being messed up by the opposition or by injuries. Observing the operation of a back-row, for example, complicated by the limitations of the players (even at international level you must allow for that), the particular range of problems posed by the opposition, different purposes in different parts of the field, and the need to keep an eye on four players – for the scrum-half is an honorary member of the back row – all this may tax the most experienced observer. That's an extreme case: you will be able to work out a greater number of formal factors using the first method.

You also have recourse to your *local coaching committee*, and to *Union coaching advisors*. Wherever possible, try to give advance notice of the questions you want to ask: nobody has immediate access to some official encyclopaedia. On the other hand, you should certainly try to get them to be specific in indicating what they recommend and *why* they recommend it. Once again, if you can get an idea of the principle behind their answers, you may be able to adapt it to your needs.

The same thing holds good of *courses* at every level. All too often courses depend on the expertise of the actual course members, with the staff limiting their role to organisation. This can rarely be justified, especially at national level, and can lead to embarrassing scenes, as when a genuine expert suddenly appears and demolishes what the course members have been patiently building. Of course, it would be more embarrassing if it had been the staff coaches who were doing the building. You're entitled to better treatment than that, and you're certainly entitled to clear presentations of models and principles. So ask for them. Don't be content simply to watch a demonstration: ask what the guiding principles are. If you're asked to serve on courses, ask what your topic will be and prepare your material so that you can give clear answers on those lines.

Then you have *books* on coaching. You should be able to make the same demands on them: before you take them out of the library, or out of the bookshop, check that they're dealing in adequate detail with the areas that interest you, and that they're advancing principles.

But much the most interesting way forward is to use all of these sources as spurs to *personal exploration*: take seriously your own ability to identify principles and to devise models. Remember: you rarely if ever start from scratch. You can make initial progress by reorganising and rearticulating what you already know. How much of the following is really new?

Back-row defence at a midfield scrum: principle/form

- We must cover against overload/so scrum-half and right flanker take the near side; No. 8 and left flanker, the far side.

- We must check close attack/so first available player takes first attacker.

- We must stop them crossing the gain line/so we must drive forward to meet them.

- We mustn't get outflanked/so if we have to cross over, we cross behind our scrum.

But if your players grasp these principles, they can respond flexibly to a variety of situations that you could not possibly treat individually. Moreover, once you and the players have clarified the principles, you can work together to devise forms of action appropriate to their own abilities.

You'll find, too, that one thing leads to another. Once you've thought about the need not to be outflanked, when players cease to be of any use in defence, you can go on to work out more precise models to curb the excesses of your flanker who is obsessed with a desire to knock down fly-halves. Time after time he charges at them; time after time they spin the ball away and he is lost. He lacks a grasp of the principles of running in the loose (which he'll find in *Total Rugby*, p. 302 ff.), and he lacks a model of when to attack the fly-half. Again, is there anything radical in this?

- Commit yourself to the fly-half only when the odds are in your favour.

There's your principle, and it's precise: you don't ignore him at any time, but you don't go for him unless the odds are with you. So what tilts the odds?

- when their pack is under heavy pressure;
- when the ball is wet;
- when the wind is strong in your face;
- when the scrum-half is weak;
- when the fly-half is having a bad day;
- when you are near their goal-line;
- when you might smother a kick.

And he ends up with a model that gives real guidance, and covers a range of situations that, again, you couldn't treat individually.

So far, we've looked at two types of model: what we might call *technical* – relating directly to mechanical techniques; and *organisational* – in which we try to give guidance to team members. There's a third type, which is basically *tactical*. It's equally simple to understand, and to construct. It's based on the predictability of opposing defensive formations. If you were asked to draw a diagram of defence from a tactical point, you'd do it without problems. You'll see a typical example at the beginning of Chapter 4, and there you'll see how these models can be turned to technical advantage. Try this one for yourself: a scrum, our put-in, on the intersection of our 10m line and the right-hand 15m line. There's a wind at our back. As soon as you draw this, you'll see that their left winger has problems. From that position, it's likely that we'll kick . . . but if he goes back to cover that, it opens up an ideal situation for blind-side attack. You'll see later just how important recurrent situations can be in simplifying the job of the tactical decision-makers.

I've tried to show you how this way of organising knowledge works, and how simple it is to get started. You start with what you already know. By thinking about it in this way, you'll mobilise your experience and make it more accessible. As you go on, it'll prompt you to develop new knowledge. Once you start doing it, you'll enjoy it: it can become a minor art form that is quite absorbing as well as immensely useful to your team. And to start, all you need to do is select a topic that interests you and start doodling.

'Doodling' because we're not dealing with big events: we're trying to come up with helpful ideas for a team playing a game. Some people get very worried about introducing their own ideas. I remember a headmaster asking me: 'Where do you get the courage to try your ideas?' It hadn't struck me that courage was involved: it seemed natural to try to improve things. But if you are worried:

- consider that the vast majority of new ideas in rugby start with someone just like you, with equal doubts and fears. Institutions don't have ideas – indeed, they cast a blight on those in their shadow. *People* have ideas;
- think it through carefully: there's no great pressure;
- talk it over with the players – let them help develop it;
- introduce it gradually, player by player, bit by bit;
- don't get emotionally involved in it. There's no need to nail your colours to the masthead. If it doesn't work, try something else.

STEP TWO: REFINE OUR RESPONSE TO FEEDBACK

Feedback is the information that can be derived from the results of a given performance. Properly interpreted, it's the basis for improving the quality of later performances.

The process is a part of everyday life. You'll see a sophisticated form of it as a competent salesman modifies his approach in response to a potential client's comments and body language. Any good speaker or teacher uses it constantly as he responds to his audience. We all use it, but we have to learn how to apply it on a more conscious level to rugby. We have to observe carefully the results of a particular action, and then link it to the principles in our model. It's absolutely essential in improving individual techniques. A typical example is goal-kicking. This is described at length in *Total Rugby* (p. 153 ff.), but a simple example will be enough here: if the player kicks, and the ball swings off to the right, reference to the principles immediately suggests that his foot, instead of swinging through the ball on the desired line of flight, has swung across it from right to left. So instead of saying 'try again', the coach can give specific advice on how to avoid the fault.

Organisationally, the same kind of thing holds true. We've been spinning the ball wide, and our fly-half has been watching the opposition response. They start to use a drift defence – there's our feedback. So he calls for a straight switch with inside-centre to check the drift.

Tactically, the scrum-half is watching the progress of our pack. We've been driving on up front, with the scrum-half feeding players who have dropped off. Soon, the opposition begin to fringe to cover that danger. At that point, guided by feedback, he calls for a continued drive in the maul.

The whole thing is basically common sense, and players pick it up fast. I remember working with an Argentinian scrum-half and an audience of 90 players (I'd asked for nine, but the message got distorted) in the basement of a soccer stadium in Cordoba, and the growing excitement as they *all* began to read the feedback and coach him. The first thing is to focus their attention on it. Some players find it hard to examine what they've messed up: they hang their heads, and look at the ground. Be positive with them: the way to improve is to work out what you did wrong and put it right next time. Besides which, it's a game we're involved in; nobody's going to die because of it.

The clues you're looking for can vary in scale. Working on a clinic skill, it may be as slight as a failure to get the length you want on a throw-in; in team organisation, it may take in feedback from the entire pack distributed over the field. In all cases, it's handy if the players try to check when you tell them to and to hold their position. For example, you've set up an exercise in defensive support for your pack (*Total Rugby*, p. 304). At an appropriate point you blow the whistle and they check their movement as quickly as they safely can. Then you talk them individually and collectively into taking precise note of the feedback available to them. Go through the components of the model: ask them about the cover they're offering the man ahead; the cover they themselves are getting; whether the line they're running on was accurate relative to the movement of the ball; what they did when the attacking line did a miss move; and so on. You can't talk to everyone each run, so to pinpoint your focus use your own expectations of who'll need help; and remember, you can always say something – praise the player when your expectation of weakness is wrong.

It's easy in your practices to offer precise feedback:

- offer a precise measure of success – throw to a mark on the wall; kick at a single post; follow through down a line on the ground. It never hurts to demand more precision in practice than will be needed in the match;

- time what they do – in establishing fitness standards; in spinning the ball to the wing; in the sprints the forwards do between scrums in a sequence of practice scrums. Players respond well to target times;

- measure what they do – how far they moved the ball on the last timed run; how far they drove their partner back in practice rucking-contact;

- monitor individuals – get a reserve to assess the line of run; the number of steps with the ball; the running speed of his rival in the first XV. That spurs both players to higher levels of concentration.

Indeed, all these devices don't just inform – they motivate.

The other great use of feedback is to prompt you to refine your model of an activity. It can be disconcerting when your model doesn't help you to put right a fault, but it does mean that you've identified a point where you can improve that model. I remember in my very early days working with a scrum-half on Teeside. He'd obviously thought as hard as I had about the principles of passing off the ground, and looked convincing, but there was a remarkable lack of power. That was the feedback. I got him to do a series of passes while I applied Method One, working through doggedly. He and the audience were getting restive, when it struck me like a minor revelation: he was following through straight down the line with both hands. Analogies with javelin throwing leapt to mind. A moment later, my model of passing was significantly altered by a new principle: to accelerate shoulder rotation the non-passing arm had to swing away from the desired line of flight. It was good for me and for the player; it was good for the audience too – they saw a coach really puzzled, and thinking out an answer. From then on, my expectation was that if there was a lack of power I should look first at the free arm.

All went well, until I met another player whose pass lacked power, even though, to my irritation, his free arm was working properly. Once again, we went back to Method One, and a sequence of passes, until I noticed that his rear knee was touching the ground early in the weight shift, stopping it dead each time and effectively killing the pass. We still had to find out why his knee touched the ground, but that didn't take long: he was overextending the front leg. So, once again, feedback from performance made it easy to improve later performance and helped to refine my model and my expectations. Now, when I came across a lack of power, I had two things to check out.

The players I've mentioned shared this experience. They, too, learned a new principle and refined their models. If later, in a match, they lost power on the pass, they'd have clear expectations of what they'd done wrong, and could concentrate on not doing it again. Broadly speaking, to miss one kick at goal may be a misfortune; to miss two begins to smack of carelessness.

You can see, though, that if the player is to benefit from feedback he has to be prepared for it. It would take an exceptional person to work out the implications of a mistake and the necessary means to put it right in the heat of the match.

It is clear that feedback, properly interpreted, leads to expectations of the best action to take in a particular case, and it's to the expectations that we turn next.

STEP THREE: CLARIFYING OUR EXPECTATIONS

Expectations form the sharp end of the whole method. If we can reduce to expectations all that we learn from the method, we can work fast and accurately as coaches and players.

Once we've established a connection between effect and cause – seen it work several times, as in the case of the powerless pass – we can make a virtually instantaneous diagnosis of that mistake, and, as a corollary, supply an effective treatment. Once we've established a probable effect from a cause – we've reached this point on the field, and so their defence is likely to be weak *there* and *there* – we can make fast, effective decisions on where to target our next strike. And because we've established these tactical probabilities, we've worked out how best our team could exploit them. Once again, we can take effective action.

Expectations work for us because 95% of our experience is consistent. The other 5% we can worry about when it occurs. In the heat of the practice, or the higher temperature of the match, to be able to make good decisions fast 95% of the time is invaluable.

Of course, we go on refining our expectations in the light of new experience. In the first minute of my first international, I looked over my shoulder at a line-out to see the last Frenchman half-way across the pitch; there was no way he could get the ball. Then the winger threw in, and I discovered that my expectation was wrong. Years later, after injury, I had to prove my fitness, and played in a minor game where I discovered that most of my expectations were wrong at that level. Expectations work best in an accustomed setting: a shift of milieu means relearning, and refining our expectations.

It's obvious that this is again part of our everyday experience. Colin, who runs the village garage, traces down faults with speed and accuracy – he has models of our car systems, is finely tuned in to feedback, has expectations of what's probably responsible for each symptom, and expectations of what treatment will put it right. It's because he has reduced his experience to expectations that he can work so efficiently. We all of us exercise this approach in some aspect of our life. We'd all gain if we could apply it to the game of rugby.

I'm pretty sure that gifted coaches and players already do, without feeling a need to articulate it. The player who 'reads the game' well is a player whose expectations are accurate. They allow him to be consistently ahead of play. The coach who runs a sequence of unopposed, and then surprises the players by identifying six or seven specific points to be put right, is employing the same method: his expectations allow him to focus on the points that will *probably* require attention. He, too, is ahead of play.

The gifted player has two built-in advantages: he *believes* in his expectations (because they work); and his mind keeps functioning calmly in the toughest situations. Belief and commitment are necessary when doing anything in rugby: it's not a half-hearted sort of game; you've got to back your hunch. Staying calm under pressure lets you function efficiently in your reading of the game and your decision-making. The coach can encourage both qualities in players where they aren't habitual – you'll see how later in this book.

I first worked this system out in terms of coaches. When I realised it applied to players, and that it drastically simplified tactical decision-making, it felt like another minor revelation. Its importance cannot be overestimated: the whole aim of the system is to provide accurate expectations that lead to immediate effective action by coaches and players alike. For the TDM, especially, the sheer speed of employing expectations is critical. He has no time to scan the whole field; his attention must be directed to what is likely to be significant. Without that, even at international level, you still see (I saw one the other day) a scrum-half receiving the ball without the slightest idea of what he is going to do with it. He isn't controlling events; he is being overwhelmed by them.

STEP FOUR: CHECK YOUR EXPECTATIONS IN ORDER OF PROBABILITY

If your expectations are accurate, this can be done quickly. You won't be faced by battalions of possibilities – just two or three strong probabilities.

This is true for the coach even when he is monitoring an apparently complicated sequence of programmed unopposed. He has dictated the sequence, and for each element in the sequence will have one or two expectations of weakness. All he has to do is focus on those expectations, and check them out. At the end of the sequence he has hard fact to offer: praise if they've done well; coaching help if skill has let them down; appropriate comment if they're not going hard enough. You'll see that his expectations may be of two kinds: he has a set of expectations based on his knowledge of the game, and a set based on his knowledge of these particular players. Which he uses at any particular point goes back to his own sense of priorities.

Your TDM – who is a representative figure, for the whole team should be thinking on the same lines – can't handle more than a few possibilities. His expectations direct his observation of the opposing defence: he doesn't have to sift through loads of material. His expectations direct him to what's most likely to be significant. The order in which he looks will almost certainly be conditioned by what he and the team like to do. At a given situation there may be two possibilities: his choice will probably reflect his sense of team strengths.

The selector has his viewing focused by his expectations: at the end of the match he would like to have his hopes/doubts resolved on perhaps four aspects of the player's game. He may well be able to check on all four without establishing a list of priorities – if, for example, they are associated with separate facets of play. If they're not, then he'll scan in order of probable importance to the team. (You'll find this discussed at length later.)

The referee is faced by the same need for fast and accurate decisions as the TDM. This is true of his personal movement round the pitch, and of his handling of the play situations. As he approaches a line-out, for example, he has expectations based on general rugby practice, the particular teams involved, and the regional refereeing culture of which he's a product. There are quite striking regional differences, even within England, less in the interpretation of the laws than in the priority accorded to them. Since they reflect the expectations of a body of referees dealing with local players over a long time, they provide perhaps the most appropriate guide. The trouble comes when you have matches involving teams from different traditions. Establishing a general consensus on priorities before international tournaments is now accepted. That apart, you can see that expectations will direct the referee's attention to what seems probable and that his priority in checking will dictate the order in which he does so. (This may give a false impression: despite looking for specific problems, he'll respond to conspicuous misbehaviour wherever it occurs.)

STEP FIVE: CHOICE OF ACTION

To a great extent, the choice of action is implicit in the proper working of the method. The coach working on a technique relates the weakness to a principle, and in doing so recognises the need to reapply that principle. He may have to consider if there is a particular case for departure from the principle, but, once solved, that too is built into his expectations. An example will help to make this *clear*.

(a) A scrum-half is blocking. You explain that this is an error. He passes again, and blocks again: he knows what he is trying to do, but he can't carry it out.

(b) If the coach is puzzled, it's because he hasn't built the concept of balance into his model. In reaching forward for the ball, or in bending forward over a straight leg, the scrum-half's centre of gravity has moved too far in front of his feet. Blocking is the alternative to falling forward.

(c) The coach explains, and the player puts it right at once.

In the same way, the TDM who has reached a particular situation has expectations of where the team can attack. In practices, he and the team have examined the possibilities and worked out how best to exploit them. They've practised intensively the form of attack that seems best. Of the possibilities, one is very appropriate to the team's strength, and that's the one likely to be chosen unless the opposition have shown that they too are strong in combating that form of attack. So the choice of action is moderately easy and likely to be effective. Remember, too, that players employing this method will be ahead of play, and that all the players will respond to an understood and possibly predicted call. There's nothing here of the panic-stricken scrum-half who gets the ball without any idea of how to use it. You'll find this approach developed in detail in Integrated Tactical Development.

THE COACH AND THE PLAYER

More often than not, the player, in pre-coaching times and even now, has been left to work out his repertoire of answers to opportunities or dangers on the spur of the moment, with his speed of improvement governed by his own capacity to assimilate his experience. The gifted player has been able to apply good normal mental habits to the game: he has learned early that it pays to think, and especially to think ahead. Very often, it's this kind of ability which fits him for central decision-making roles. What he's doing is what most people learn to do in one field or another. You use it unconsciously, for example, every time you drive your car, though at the start it all seemed strange and difficult.

As I drive in to work, I come to a busy roundabout. I have a clear *model* of how I'm going to get across it: I'm going to approach in a given lane, and I get into it early; I know exactly where I'm going to start signalling on the way across; I 'know' the speeds I'll use. I also know exactly what to look for in terms of opportunity and danger. These are my *expectations*, and I concentrate on them. For that moment, I'm not considering the university tower looming up ahead, or the trees, or the sky: I'm checking people queuing to cross, and traffic coming from the right. I've worked out ready *answers* for opportunities and problems, in terms of our abilities (mine and my car's).

Your gifted player behaves just like that on the pitch. As is always the case, we're trying to encourage the less gifted to behave in the same way as the gifted. The gifted player feels it's obvious, it's 'natural', and usually imagines that everyone is doing the same thing. At a certain level they already are, but they need to be encouraged to do so consistently, and helped to do so accurately.

Both 'thinking' and 'thinking ahead' are encouraged by the suggested method. Thinking is what happens when the player begins to monitor his own performance, pick out what he did or is doing wrong, and work to put it right. Thinking ahead can be long term – when the player goes in for mental rehearsal before the match, checking over difficult situations, getting the model clearer, getting the expectations more precise, checking the cues that will indicate the action, and working out how best to meet the situation. It can also – and this is where speed is essential – be short term: how is/are he/they/the team/opposition going to handle the developing situation, here, in the next moment, in the match? This is when accurate expectations are all-important.

The more we encourage our players to organise their knowledge in terms of model, feedback, expectations, scanning and action, the better it will be for them and for us. We want players who contribute positively to their own development, and to the development of the team; who can monitor their own performance and that of their team, and get rid of weaknesses. We want them to adopt the same habits of mind that we seek in ourselves. We want them to understand what they're doing, and to aim always to do it better.

Together, we want to work for the future – a future in which the individual player, the units and the team all improve. But we mustn't lose sight of the need to play to our present strengths. If I drive as if my car is a Ferrari, when in fact it's an elderly VW, I can get into deep trouble. So we must work as players and coach to improve our standards of performance even in the simplest things. We must seek to eliminate mistakes, as only by doing that can we hope to develop more enterprising team play. All our planning must be based on what we can deliver.

How best can we help the player? How best can he help himself?

As you coach him, make clear the principles on which you want him to work
Principles liberate. Once he has grasped principles, he can cope with wide variations of application. Principles are components of the models you build up. Consider defensive covering in the loose. It's pointless drawing lines; it's pointless telling your No. 8 to corner-flag; he needs principles.

- Get your head up early; guess what's going to happen; back your hunch.
- You're aiming to get between the ball and our line, as far forward as you safely can.
- Run off the man ahead of you, covering his weakness: if he's going out too fast, cover him inside; it he's going too far forward, run deeper.
- Run with a sense of the need to get width and depth about the axis of attack.
- If you're the lead man, and they look like doing a switch, go with the ball-carrier and leave the man coming in to the rest of the pack.

Most of these are self-explanatory, but make sure that they are understood as rational solutions to rational problems. The more mysteries there are, the worse you are coaching.

Encourage him to interpret feedback
To be effective, he must constantly monitor his own performance. As he gallops across the field in defensive covering, he'll be varying his line and varying his speed as he responds to the opposition. They do a miss move, he immediately runs deeper; they're slow on a pass, he shades forward.

As coach, you need to make him very aware of the need to pick up as many clues as possible. So, too, with his own performance: he must check and interpret. He has to trace cause from effect: 'I was outflanked by the fly-half, so . . .'; 'My pass curled in behind the receiver, so . . .'; 'I came through on that switch running in rather than straight, so . . .'. The clearer the model you give him, and the clearer the principles on which it's based, the easier his task becomes: 'I've got to run flatter'; 'I've got to check rotation on the hand behind the ball'; 'I've got to lie deeper initially'.

You start the process in practices where you provide *clear criteria of success and failure*. You want your thrower-in to throw accurately? Put a chalk mark on the wall, so that he can see clearly what he has done, and correct it. You want your goal-kicker to win matches for you? Get him kicking from the goal-line at a single post. You want fast, positive support? Insist on flat passes in all practices, and count how many strides the ball-carrier has to take before he can pass flat to the weak supporter. It takes a little longer to work out beforehand, but accurate feedback is at the heart of personal development.

Crystallise his discoveries into expectations

Encourage your players to take mental note of each deduction of cause from effect, or effect from cause; in their case as in yours, expectations, if soundly based, accelerate effective action.

Let him see you experiment to find effective answers

When problems come up, it's really helpful to let the player take part in solving them – there's a section about this just below. He's got to see trial and error at work as you think your way towards a solution. He's got to realise that rugby is no more esoteric than any other part of ordinary life, and that you work out solutions in a sensible way.

Most of this is a matter of manner, of approach: read the section on encouraging problem-solving immediately below. But the aim, of course, is to render the player capable of coaching himself, and in due course of coaching others. A step on this way is his becoming unit leader.

What the general method means for the unit leader

Every unit is an aggregate of individuals; you don't coach 'a scrum' but the eight individuals within it. What you say goes into eight sets of ears, and is processed by eight separate brains. You monitor individual performance, and make individual corrections. Yes, you can make blanket appeals and pronouncements, but at the end of the day you're working with individual players.

However, you certainly must have a model of unit performance – your plan of how the unit is going to co-operate to a given end. You will have clear expectations of what (in general terms) or who (in terms of your players) is most likely to go wrong. And you provide more or less ready answers for what you spot. You can't be there to do it on the field of play – so you need someone who will.

The technical role of the leader is to act as the coach on the field, checking on concentration and checking on performance. To do this, he too has to cultivate the mental attitudes of the coach, and the same method of scanning. The more he is made *in practices* to see the whole picture, understand the principles behind the model, recognise the likely problems in execution, adopt quality standards and constantly apply them, and get used to sorting out solutions for the problems, the more likely he is to do it on the field.

One particular case of leading is that of the TDM, and his role is so central to the enterprising use of the ball that much of the third part of this book uses him as a critical example for the preparation of the individual player. He more than anyone else needs the speed and accuracy of action which the system promotes.

How to encourage problem-solving

The idea that every player is his own best coach leads naturally – though not inevitably – to a set of three related coaching techniques which will help reinforce that central idea.

1. Coaching by objectives

Players respond best when they've a target to aim for. If you identify realisable targets for each player, you'll find greater commitment to achieving them.

This starts off with the end-of-season preparations for the following season: a coach/senior players conference; the sketching out of probable teams; and the identification of problems faced by each player. Why is B the second-choice fullback? What does he have to do to improve his game? What help will he need?

These targets will change as the player improves, but the general model for individual players and group and team leaders remains the same: target identification . . . target setting . . . coaching intervention.

These are best set on a weekly basis. At the team talk, try to identify the problem (though it may be less a problem than a search for greater excellence), suggest exercises and points to look for, and arrange a time for personal help. This is a fundamental way of guaranteeing progress in the individual and the team. All it takes is a little forethought.

(It has always struck me as deeply unsatisfactory that, at national level, players of great talent but with identifiable weaknesses are allowed to start the following season with the weaknesses uncorrected. A simple application by the national coach of the following method could help to eliminate the problem. A clear statement to the player; communication of methods to his club or regional coach; invitations to both to meet at the coaching conferences which all nations now run; and you convert that conference into a genuine problem-solving occasion at which all the attendant coaches are given the chance to see coaching at work on real problems. Everyone benefits.)

The more precisely the target (or the problem) is defined, the more productive the exercise becomes. 'You've got to improve your tackling' is evidently less satisfactory than 'we've got to improve the way you cut down your opponent's options when he's got space'.

The more technically it's defined the better. Keep the target within the player's control. It's useless setting 'achievement' targets like 'you've got to get into the

1st team', or letting the player delude himself with such objectives: all he can do is his best to improve his performance, and all the coach can do is help him to focus his efforts. Certainly, the coach can underline his potential as a player, and set him appropriate quality standards, but he must also explain that being selected is something that happens to you, not something you can guarantee by your efforts.

2. Heuristic coaching

Self-coaching implies problem-solving – at its simplest: observing results and working out how to improve them. The coach's whole approach can reinforce this or inhibit it. He reinforces it by asking questions that the player can answer; he inhibits it by imposing answers without explanation. Every time you ask a question the player can answer, you build up his willingness to try to solve problems and you make it a little surer that he won't forget the point.

The critical factor is selecting the right question. The easiest way of starting is to draw his attention to a weakness and then offer *alternatives*: 'Should you do that . . . or that?' In fact, this is doing most of the thinking for him, but he feels as if he's doing it for himself, and therefore that he's *capable* of doing it for himself.

You can reinforce this by building in *cues* – by the tone of your voice, for instance, or the way you shift your hand or your weight.

If he gives the wrong answer, take it and get him to consider the *implications*. 'So you reckon if . . . then . . .?' Most of the time, if your original question was roughly right, that'll do the trick.

A further useful tool is to present the player with *analogies* – prompting him to solve the new problem by comparing it with an understood previous experience. For example, the fullback who wants to learn to drop-kick will be helped if he's prompted to think of it as a place-kick, with the main problem being to put the ball down in exactly the same position (relative to the non-kicking foot) and attitude (relative to the ground) as for the place-kick. Give him a working partner to check on these particular points, and then add questions about balance, contact with the ball, and line of follow-through. Or perhaps you've been working on making all your back row into competent stand-in scrum-halves, at least as far as their spin-pass off the ground is concerned. It's then extraordinarily easy to use their understanding of that to teach them to screw-kick really accurately – the model is mechanically almost identical.

These potential analogies come from inside the game, but you can use parallels from any field, from track and field to guerrilla warfare. Gradually you'll find that you don't need to simplify to the same extent: he has started thinking for himself.

Later on, with more experienced players, there are big benefits to the coach in asking open questions: 'What do you think we should do about this?' You may have a clear answer in mind, but you'll find that their ideas may enhance and refine your own, and at the least you'll see the kind of explanation that's going to be needed in presenting your own solution.

Heuristic coaching – *an apprentice hooker sorts out his style*

This is a fairly typical case. You ask questions, and you invite the player to experiment in finding an answer. Where necessary you give clues. For example, when you ask if he'll get a faster strike from the hip or the knee, you show him a ponderous movement of the whole of your leg, then flick from the knee. When you ask him how he would extend his strike, you grab his foot and pull till the left knee bends . . . and he learns to bend his left knee. Build in enough body language and you can have a kid who's never hooked striking like an international (within the limits of his own response times) in a few minutes – *and* he will have a better opinion of his own ability to solve problems. This is a technical case, but, if your own model is clear, you can direct any player's attention to any aspect of play and he'll come up with answers. If he doesn't, you've not tailored the question to fit.

We'll start off with the hooker by himself, leaning against a chair, with both hands on the seat. The back of the chair is to his left. Don't keep him down too long: get him up for a rest every couple of questions.

- Do you want your weight on your right or left foot?
- Do you want your left foot across nearer the ball, or further away?
- Do you want it further forward or further back?
- Do you want your right knee pointing at the ball or away from it?
- Do you get a faster movement from your hip or from your knee?
- Do you want your right side up or down?
- How do you extend your strike?
- Do you want your striking leg tight or relaxed?
- Do you want your right shoulder high or low?
  What will that do to your opponent?
  So should he get further away from you or closer?
  So what should that tell you?

OK. Here's the ball: we'll put it directly under the loose-head's inside shoulder. Do you want it parallel to the tunnel, at right angles to the tunnel, or pointing obliquely towards you?

Good. You're going to strike for it, but you need a target. The target is the No. 8's feet. We'll get him to put his hands where he wants the ball. Now concentrate on the line of the strike. Do you want your striking foot ending up against your left foot, or going through towards the No. 8?

OK: try a few strikes. When I touch the ball, you strike like a rattlesnake. Fine, but a lot of these went well to the left of the No. 8. Do you need to strike deeper or shallower? Remember, it's going to be very competitive: do you want to strike at the ball or beyond it? Occasionally, you're trying to turn your foot. Is that a strong movement or a weak movement?

OK, now lower your right hip and strike for the ball with your heel and Achilles tendon. Is that a strong movement or a weak movement? Well, try it: I'll try to hold the ball against it. Good. Now I'm going to move the ball further away – further than you'll need to strike in the match. How are you going to get to it? You worked that out earlier, remember?

OK, back to the normal position with the ball. When I touch it, you strike – and this time aim at the ball, not at my hand.

Good – but we need more speed. See this 2p piece? I'm going to drop it from hip-high: you've got to hook it before it hits the ground. And now from a little lower . . . and a little lower. Very good. Now we'll bring in your props:

- if you're going to be closer to one than the other, which one will it be?
- do you want the loose-head to bind at your armpit or your hips?
- do you want the tight-head's left side high or low?
- and the loose-head's right side?
- do you want your hips trapped between theirs? so how will you go down?

You can see that, asking the right questions, you could get him to model not just everything about the front row, but about the locks: where they push; where their feet should be; what should happen when the ball gets stuck in the second row; what he should see when he looks back; and so on. That's because the whole scrum has evolved as a set of answers to precisely these questions, or the problems behind them.

Getting him to answer *all* the questions takes longer than telling him answers. But getting him to answer the questions lets him coach himself when you're not there, and makes him a little more willing to work out answers to other questions – not necessarily to do with rugby. So you find a reasonable compromise. Once you've coached him, get him to repeat the process with other potential hookers: it spreads knowledge and reinforces his own understanding.

You'll see that the questions have helped him to create a model of hooking; that he's getting directed to important feedback that leads to expectations of how to cope with problems. And you don't need to mention a single one of those words.

I hope you've done the same. If not, the questions were a shade too hard. If I had been with you, I would have been reshaping them as soon as we'd had a long pause. You'll find a working model of hooking in *Total Rugby* (pp. 189–91). Most importantly, however, you can see that the apparently mysterious art of hooking is eminently understandable, like the rest of the game.

3. Quality control and total quality control

Coaching is all about quality control. It's about ensuring that whatever is being produced – a place-kick, or the timing of the shove, or the selection of a focus of attack – is being produced adequately. As soon as we introduce the idea of self-coaching, we transfer in part the quality-control function to the player. We provide him with a model, with expectations of what may go wrong, and with a habit of monitoring his own performance. We also provide him with appropriate standards of performance. If you can convince him that his future development depends on the standards of quality control that he imposes on himself, you're on your way to producing a self-regulating player. If you can do it with your team, you're on your way to TAC – the Japanese system whereby the worker and not merely the management accepts responsibility for his contribution to the quality of the total product – in your case, effective team play.

Creating an effective atmosphere

Much of this book is about getting players to use their judgement in an intelligent way. For some coaches this will be difficult: I've known coaches who wouldn't hold an open team-meeting for fear questions would come up that they couldn't answer. Yet if we can get beyond this unreal notion that a coach has to be infallible, the contribution by the players can transform the team. One way of doing this is to hold team meetings in which every player in turn has his say. This will function better, however, if there's a consistent openness about relationships within the whole group. Some simple ideas will encourage the basic trust that's needed.

- *Respect the players and encourage them to respect each other*
  The most fruitful approach is to assume that everyone is doing his best but would like to do better. Be conscious of the players as people; try to be aware of how they see themselves, and try to give them what they need. This isn't in the least opposed to brisk, effective work – simply build it into your overall approach.

- *Lead them, don't just tell them*
  The true leader creates an atmosphere in which people want to do what he wants them to do. If the players believe that you respect them, and see that you listen to them and have realistic plans for making them and the team better, and if you put your heart and head into it, you're well on the way. Stay real. Don't get dogmatic when you're not sure; over-confident when you're scared; aggressive when you've no ideas. You don't need to be 'one of the boys' – the search for high standards should set you apart and mark you out functionally.

  Leadership is a skill at which you need to work, not a position or a state. It's a skill in the art of presentation. You imagine how best to appeal to them – how the task can be made most desirable in their eyes. You offer what you want in a context that will excite and satisfy them. You adopt a role that lets *them* adopt satisfying roles. Obviously no single role will cover all situations, but these are powerful inducements:

  – that they are special;

  – that they've a touch of heroism, to fight against the odds;

  – that they can be proud of each other in terms of skill, enterprise and effort;

– that people expect much of them;

– that they have special roles in the team;

– that they have special roles in the game;

– that they have special abilities.

It's a blend of complimenting them for what they are, and for what you and they would like them to be. It's addressed to them as a group, and to them as individuals. It's implicit in the standards you set them.

Just as the good captain dramatises his purpose, so does the good coach; whatever he's 'really' like, he needs to be a little larger than life in his coaching. His energy, drive, commitment and vision of what can and should be done condition these elements in the players: he must be convincing. But this is a truism: the successful man believes in what he's doing.

- *Encourage open communication*
The great imperative is to get the players contributing to the team – talking to you, talking seriously about how to sort out, problem by problem, what stands between the team and the top. You want to promote this in terms of the mini-teams inside the team. It's astonishing how little effort players make to communicate: they're often inhibited by a feeling that they've no right to interfere.

Keep the actual discussion off the practice field if you possibly can. Try to get it done after the match or before the practice session begins: once you're on the field you want intensive work rather than talk.

- *Delegate responsibility*
No coach can take care of a team adequately by himself. He needs to build up a system of delegation in which players accept responsibility for their own sections of the team. It's evident throughout this book that team functioning calls for central control of decisions, central control of standards. To do this you need people accustomed to functioning as coach-substitutes; people who'll represent the coach on the field during the match. You need a forward leader who casts the same perceptive eye over the line-out as the coach does, and who puts things right, just as the coach does. For him, it's part of his growth and development. You give him a list of what's to be done in practices, and talk it over with him beforehand. You make it clear that he's in charge, and responsible to you. You make it clear that you believe he can do it. While you're actually there with the forwards, you make very clear the thinking behind what you're doing, and the methods you're employing. And you do this for each mini-unit.

This has to be compatible with their own personal attitudes: you've got to feel that each is going to function in a way analogous to your own. I've never, but once, had difficulties in getting the right person, because I start assessing potential leaders long before I'm going to need them, and create an acceptance of them before they're appointed.

- *Be personally organised*

  The least you can do for the players who let you take over hours of their time in an activity they prize is to appear organised on the field. It's one indication of how you respect them. After years and years of coaching, I still think very hard about what I'm going to do, write it down, carry the paper with me. You'll find that it's a major help to adopt a structure for your sessions – not a crushing, inhibiting structure that totally controls you, but an *aide-memoire* that brings coherence and inclusiveness to your work. I've already written about this at some length in *Total Rugby* (pp. 72–7).

- *Work for the individual*

  I've never met a player who didn't deeply appreciate help with his personal playing development. It's the ultimate technical guarantee of the respect in which he's held. It's also the most lasting satisfaction in coaching. The point I've made about the detailed observation of match performance is the key to this; though, of course, you see a lot in practices. The first question I ask new players has always been: 'What are you bad at?' – for it's my job to put that right as far as I can. And, of course, this desire to strengthen the individual is the real key to team development. You're always working through individuals, getting individuals to modify their behaviour: you don't change a team, you change individual players in the team. You can do this far more effectively if

  > ### Fig. 1 The structured session: a worked example
  >
  > The illustration is a 'used' structured session, retrieved from under piles of paper. You can see how it's planned: intensive handling; individual skill (turning an opponent and what to do when turned); unit work (myself taking the backs and my good friend Toshi the forwards, with a detailed programme of what to cover); unopposed team practices (including, at c and d, thematic unopposed); short sharp opposed sessions against the reserves.
  >
  > What you can't see is the planning, and the purpose. It's directed at getting rid of weaknesses, for example, iii. 4 is aimed at learning how to deal with an extra man coming through the centre against us – and I can still remember why we had to practise it. The turning exercises at 2 reflect another point that had to be improved.
  >
  > You can guess, too, what the forwards were concentrating on by looking at what they had to be able to do in iv. a, c and d, and v. d. The whole practice is being tested out in that last 25 minutes, against an opposition keen to defeat us.
  >
  > Capital letters are a signal to me – 'don't forget . . .': whatever else I get across, I have to get that over. The written notes imply tie-up points about players: Kotetsu and his hamstring; Hashi, the reserve scrum-half working closely with Ota, the player in possession; Kane and Taira – the fullback and a lock – being reminded of the need to function as coach and leader in our absence. The strange codes at iv. d are simply line-out formations, each letter representing a player.
  >
  > Remember that this doesn't show the working – the little notes and diagrams serving to clarify my priorities – or the energy and pace of the presentation; the planning is only as good as the preparation and the implementation.

INTETSU - *GET VERY WARM*   *HASHI - STAY WITH OTA*
TAIRA + KANE MUST <u>LEAD</u>   *loop on .. .. on the ditch*
i. handling....warm..stretch

         ordinary...over the shoulder...wide
         1-5   *TWICE REVVED*)

ii. turning in 4s in grids   nb turn-take
                       turn-fold..<u>get the ball</u> x 8 each

iii. units....forwards Toshi

           backs: 1.   back 3 + Mori: kick and catch
                       Ota..Kin..Hoso: spin

              ·   2.   check positions 4 QUALITY runs

                                        STRAIGHT CENTRES
× det } ↙   3.   rhythm - miss 3 * attack blind..miss 2 * attack blind
                                +SUPPORT WINGER
             ·   4.   get 2nd XV centres + fh: front three v extra man
                        + *fh*
                                     + Kane lying wider

WALK
SLOW   i. look at own man + fb
FAST   ii. call 'in' - OK
                          outside - <u>Kane</u> wide,<u>Kin</u> + <u>Ota</u> across
                        'out' if fh moves ball fast ..all 3 move over
iv. team....a. defensive..whistle + throw back: gather,get tight,Kane call
          b. KO - SPEED OF SUPPORT - <u>either</u> signal + Kin blind
                              miss + Kane

                  ALWAYS SUPPORT FOR WING BY OTHER BACK

                          - FORWARDS IMMEDIATE MAUL   [*TURN*]
                          - KANE call
         c. choice penalty...8 to forwards..1 pass..MAUL..Kane call
                       8 to backs..BACKS SUPPORT WINGER..MAUL..KANE
         d. line-out...SIMPLE CALLS...miss..KANE..support x 8
                PEEL...o   kjitSt
                       o   Skjo   x 8

         e. free..two lengths..FORWARDS MAUL IMMEDIATELY
                  Kane calls

v. opposed.....<u>3 minutes</u> (2 each)

        1. wide spin....keep stretching them + SUPPORT WINGER
           HOW MANY TIMES CAN WE FORCE THE OVERLAP?

        2. attacking kick (chip): get back and set it up + call v. PRESSURE
                            fisrt tackle in 2nd phase..new ball

        3. throw ins..through 2nd phase..then nearest touch

        4. scrum 10m out

instead of issuing blanket commandments you direct your attention to those who need it. I've heard so many times that coaches haven't time to do this. But if they always spoke primarily to individuals it would help, and if they structured their sessions effectively they would always be in a position to do so. There are bound to be times when the coach can devote himself to individuals; there are times (for example when coaching a hooker or a line-out jumper) when you can't really avoid it; there are times (for example during fitness training) when the coach should be free; there's a quarter of an hour before the rest come out or after the rest go in; there are meetings specially arranged; there are odd moments that you fill with a little specific activity rather than standing about. If the determination is there, time will be found.

It's fair to say that the players themselves should contribute to this. If they'd say 'I can't do this well enough. . . .' it would help prompt the reluctant coach. It's obviously true, however, that the best gift the coach can offer is to transfer a coaching attitude to the player so that he monitors his own performance.

TECHNICAL APPLICATIONS

1. The system and match analysis

Coaches renounce the pleasures of being entertained by rugby – they go to matches intent on learning more about their teams, and especially on checking out what has to be done in the following week(s) to strengthen their performance.

What typically distinguishes the successful coach is purposefulness: he knows, from his analysis of the previous match, what he has to do; and he knows precisely where his help is most needed. His programme will involve many elements common to all coaches. It will differ quite spectacularly in the detailed objectives towards which he's working. He'll do intensive handling, but concentrate on a few players with specific difficulties; he'll do scrumming, but he's most concerned with, for example, the exact line of the hooker's follow-through and the need for the locks not to shift their feet; he'll set up mauling practices, but he'll be concentrating, for example, on controlling the release of the ball. He'll do many other things under each heading, but he has clear, specific priorities.

In effect he has been viewing the match, complex as it is, in just the same way that he views the scrum-half passing a ball: as objectively and analytically as he can. He sees each match as a data-gathering exercise, on the basis of which he can plan ahead.

How effectively he can carry out this monitoring depends to a great extent on the number of models he has stored in his memory banks. Each model, each set of expectations, directs his attention towards significant elements in performance – significant in general importance, or specifically for the members of his team.

Good coaches are ahead of the game in exactly the same way as the good player. Given the situation, they know what to look for. This allows them to focus on what's likely to be significant before it happens. You'll see that this is exactly what was described in the way the coach watches an unopposed practice (see p. 27 above), except that he is no longer controlling the sequence, and has to depend on models with which he is familiar of each situation that arises.

Regularly, however, and especially at the beginning of the season, he'll set out to make specific observations, devoting more time to functions which particularly concern him. This gives him the chance to work out a clearer model of the function beforehand, and should be reflected in more precise coaching. But immediately, it gives him hard fact about team performance in that area.

For particular purposes – to bring his observations home to players, for example – he may commit them to paper. Numbers have more impact than simple statements of opinion. And there's no doubt that, for the coach himself, keeping a precise check may reveal facts he hadn't anticipated.

To keep recording the data you really need a simple system that allows you to make exact notes fast. Some basic guidelines I've found useful include the following:

Use your existing models and expectations
Use the work you've put into defining essential elements in performance to help you pinpoint the significant functions.

Concentrate on specifics
If you try to cover too much, you'll end up seeing nothing: follow the advice of the general method and look at one thing at a time, in order of priority. As you get more experienced, you may find you can mix first- and second-level data – locating a weakness and also accounting for it. Let that come – don't try for it at the start.

Clarify your criteria
At a very basic level it's easy to quantify exactly: you have a clear criterion for balls lost against the head. But the time will come when you're more interested in establishing, for example, how much 'good ball' your scrum-half is getting. The effort to define the phrase is another incentive to more precise thinking and coaching. In terms of recording, you may look for a simple criterion – 'scrum-half under no physical pressure'.

Keep the method of recording simple
During the match, you'll find that incidents pile up. If you try to record them, for example by drawing, you'll find it very difficult. Time spent reducing the function

to a set of elements which you can present in columns and fill in by a tick is time well spent.

Don't underestimate your power of aided recall
The temptation to try to cover too much can be kept in check once you realise that even simple recording will help you reconstruct what happened. Start simple and see if you need any greater complexity.

Don't divorce this method from other sources of information
Once you've spotted a weakness and got evidence of it, you may get better results by taking it to the players and talking it over with them – the odds are they'll be able to pinpoint the causes, or at least give you clues of where to look for them.

Here are some examples of recording that you may find useful.

(a) Scrum possession (see Fig. 2)
Record in terms of the team putting in. If the opponents put in and get slow ball, put a tick in their S column; if we lose the ball, put a tick in our L column; if they are penalised at put-in, put a tick in their PI column. If you use lined paper, you can use a separate line for each scrum – which will give evidence of changing trends during the game.

our ball				their ball			
PI	GB	S	L	PI	GB	S	L

Fig. 2 Recording scrum possession

(b) Back-row support
This illustrates a useful tip – to think of each column as a continuum with very good on the left, very bad on the right. In Fig. 3, flanker 7 was slow to start – he hung around when he should have gone – but ran fast to get across. (When you discuss it with him, you bring out the advantages of starting early and being able to run in balance.) His line of run was fairly optimistic – he went a little too far forward for comfort; if he'd been pessimistic he'd have gone too deep, and if he'd earned a tick precisely in the middle, he'd have been dead realistic/right. His immediate action has to be judged by results – and referred perhaps to the

judgement system described below on pp. 61–2. In this case he went straight in, fell on the ball, got up with it, and set up a ruck 15m further on.

No. & speed		line of run		immediate action	
start	running	optimistic	pessimistic	good	bad
7 *	*		*	*	

Fig. 3 Recording back-row support

You will see how much this means to the player concerned – it gives him direct personal coaching. And, of course, it helps prepare a further model, a further set of expectations for the coach.

took ball in	kept it clear	timed release	ball available
12	*	*	*

Fig. 4 Recording ball retention

I won't multiply these examples: they're easy to draw up and useful even if they function only as a simple *aide-memoire*. For example, what picture does Fig. 4 conjure up to check with your memory of the event?

Your left centre went into a tackle (you'll remember it), and kept the ball away from his opponent really well. Unfortunately, he let it go at once and an opponent got his foot to it. (It could be read differently, but it'll remind you. It would be easy to refine such a form to give more precise information – whether he held it too long or too briefly in the immediate example – but it demands that much more attention, and it's doubtful if you need it.)

You can see that you might focus these examples on a single player, so that you keep tabs only on flanker 7's support play or register data on all the back row by focusing on each in turn. You can also see how useful the procedure might be to a selector, who sets out to establish answers to questions specifically related to aspects of back-row play. And wouldn't it be useful to the player to be advised by coach and selector of what exactly he had to improve to be considered for the team? Naturally, the observation would be more accurate if it extended over a single player's performance throughout the match: the further away we get from selectorial impressionism the better.

The kind of analysis we've been looking at merits the title 'match analysis' because it's concerned with performance in a particular match. As used here it is specific and diagnostic, focused on particular facets of play with the very practical aim of improving weaknesses. There's another kind of analysis, which might more exactly be termed 'game analysis'. This is general and normative and seeks to describe statistically what in fact happens in 'the game'.

You can see that this could have very important and very useful results. If we establish the factors that correlate most highly with team success, we also establish coaching priorities for a winning team. But you'll also see that this is going to be much less easy than it appears at first. Rugby is a protean organism which alters with regard to playing level and playing style, and which has to take personnel factors into account. Japanese rugby – characterised by a higher degree of commitment than I've seen anywhere else – has, it seems to me, been handicapped by its acceptance of the evident success of the coherent New Zealand pattern of play. It's easy to establish the effective priorities in that game, and to reflect that emphasis in your practices, but if you lack vital ingredients such as superior physical presence you simply cannot hope to apply it successfully except in domestic rugby.

The first caution, therefore, is to work within comparatively narrow categories. It is pointless producing norms that cover a wide range of playing levels or styles of play.

The second comes with the application of these norms. There's a danger of halting the evolution of the game, and of the players' roles in the game, by the acceptance of accidental norms that reflect the present moment's state of development and quality of players.

The third caution is that, inevitably, the norm is mediocre. It's possible to concentrate on establishing norms of performance for, say, a prop, and to disregard outstanding examples of what can be achieved. Indeed, it's possible for the norm to be used to penalise the outstanding player. I remember clearly the expression on the face of a prop describing a meeting with a long-serving chairman of national selectors. He was told he'd never play for England because he was much too active in the loose. (His performance in the tight was specifically not mentioned.) When it reaches the point of an official stereotype which calls upon him to be able to take and give 'short' passes, you can see the limitations. The only value of such a stereotype is to establish minima – and you don't get medals for reaching the qualifying standard. We owe it to our players to develop them as fully as we can; into as complete a player as possible who also happens to be a complete prop. That isn't a target we can reach, but every step along the way, provided it isn't rashly taken, is worthwhile. In this particular case I'd be the first to agree that propping ability in the tight is the first priority, and an essential qualification. But it isn't enough.

The fourth caution is against expecting novel results. Most investigation of this kind reinforces what experience suggests are the important priorities. Would you be surprised to learn that the situation most likely to lead to a try is an attacking ruck within 10m of the line?

2. The system and purposeful selection procedures

Having a model of the kind of rugby you intend to play enables you to write a basic job description for the various positions. This will not be prescriptive in the sense of limiting the abilities needed, but simply in terms of establishing essentials. The chosen player may expand your whole sense of how to develop the pattern, but he must be able to cope with the demands as envisaged at present.

The business of selection, of observing the player in action, comes back to the standard application of the basic method. You have a clear model of the performance elements you need, of the weaknesses that may be present, and you are prepared to give undivided attention to that particular player for two or three minutes several times throughout the match. Doing this will come as a revelation to the average selector. Instead of relying on rumour you will be able to quote hard fact to support your views.

Your overall team model can be refined by thinking in terms of effective performing units. Some of these – for example having a 2 jumper and a 4 jumper; having a back row that will balance the functions – are clear. But it will help if you think of complementary back three, front three, halves – indeed of all the mini-teams that function within the team. The more carefully you balance the overall team pattern with the complementarity of the mini-teams, the more effective your team will be.

Not all of the positions will necessarily be affected by your basic team model to the point where it offers absolutely clear selection guidance. But that model will certainly allow you to define the required job to the man you select – not in terms of a maximum contribution, but of essential minima. You then can monitor his performance with the same purposefulness that the method brings to all aspects of observing.

I'm convinced, incidentally, of the wisdom of using established players to help select for the vacant places. Once you've filled in your hooker, for example, you can rely on him to supply insightful comments on who should prop, and so on.

It's obviously common sense to think less in terms of a team than of a squad, and that the squad must in terms of the basic team model be homogeneous. It would be futile to have half-backs of radically different abilities and preferences as potential substitutes; it would betray a total absence of game plan, and a cavalier disregard for the needs of the other players selected. Yet it happens at the highest level.

Keep the model clear and trust in it.

These are elements in selection, but as long as they are applied mechanically they won't bring consistent success. You don't put a team together like a kit of parts. As long as you apply these ideas short term, as long as you think as a 'team changer' rather than 'team developer', as long as you separate the functions of selector and coach, the odds are against your being successful. Players are too valuable to discard: they need to have their weaknesses diagnosed and put right, and desired strengths specified and coached. All too often the selector thinks not of improvement but of change. That's why in *Total Rugby* I suggested that the prime qualification for a selector was the ability to coach the team. In Part Three you'll find a description of a more subtle, longer-term team-building process: 'The coach and selection' (p. 111).

The value of the system

You can see, I hope, how the system works. You've almost certainly been able to recognise how you already apply something like it in your work or your hobbies – wherever you're more expert than the average man. If you test it out against your playing experience, you'll see that to some extent you must have been applying something like it there. This has been an attempt to clarify it so that it functions well, and to encourage you to apply it consistently. The beauty of a system is obviously that it allows you to work systematically, and everything we do in rugby benefits from such an approach. Even when we reach the point of what for want of a better word we call *intuition* – the timing of a sidestep, the flash of coaching insight, the selection hunch – it's going to function best within a solid, sensible structure.

Part Two

The basis of team performance

Thomas Castaignède, as scrum-half

The next stage in the development of total rugby is likely to be the inter-changeability of the backs. Here you see Castaignède acting as scrum-half, and doing so very capably. Make passing off the ground a regular feature of the individual skills section of your structured session, and within minutes you'll turn out numbers of emergency scrum-halves, capable of dealing with a scrum-half pinned under a ruck. One of the finest passers off the ground I've ever seen was a winger in La Plata. He was one of a group I'd been working with to demonstrate coaching method, and he developed an excellent pass – brilliantly quick, long and accurate – within a quarter-of-an-hour.

Expanding the scope of individual skills – skills every player should possess – is a natural consequence of the idea of total rugby. Players already toy with the notion of expanding the range of their skills: the coach can formalise the setting and make them really competent.

But choose your skills carefully, and emphasise the primacy of present duties over future fancies.

2 **Strategy and tactics**

Does your team have a clear model of how it intends to play the game? Does it have clear expectations of how and where opportunities will occur? Does it know how it can best exploit those opportunities when they occur? Does it have players prepared to seize those opportunities?

STRATEGY

Your *strategy* is the broad sweep of your game; your basic style of play; the pattern of rugby for which you have prepared and which you habitually employ; the characteristic way in which you pressurise your opponents and so create opportunities. Every team that is consistently successful at any level throughout the world of rugby has adopted such a basic pattern.

The simplest way of characterising team strategy is to specify the channel (see Fig. 5) and manner in which players have been prepared for their first-phase strike, and in which they habitually do strike. Once you have that model of team play you have immediate effective criteria for selection (basic job descriptions), coaching priorities, performance analysis, direction of team development/squad development – indeed for every practical aspect of team preparation. It brings coherence and purpose to all you do.

On the field, this basic pattern of play, which will underlie all coaching sessions, provides a resource in which the whole team feels confident and capable, and thus brings an accustomed and comfortable rhythm to its play.

The implementation of the strategy raises questions which direct the coach's attention.

- How can you clear the channel in which you intend to strike?
- How can you distract attention from it?
- How can you vary the ways in which you get the ball into it?
- How can you effectively vary the ball-carrier?

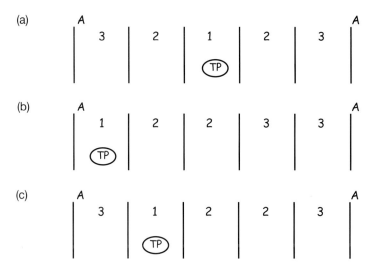

Fig. 5 Channels of attack: the basis of strategy.
These show the focus of attack in representative basic strategies.
(a) From a midfield Tactical Point
(b) From a wide TP
(c) From a TP with a workable blind-side
Key: *Channel One* (C1) is for the team that seeks to keep the ball in front of the pack, getting it there by direct forward attack; by scrum-half breaks; by bringing the ball back in and kicking high; pressurising by forward momentum; seeking the space behind the pressure defence. *Channel Two* (C2) is for the team that seeks to drive forward in the centre, retain possession, and strike for space against an off-balance and disorganised defence in the second phase. *Channel Three* (C3) is for the team that seeks to pressurise the opposition by spinning the ball wide and attacking the space on the flanks.

The success of the strategy leads to complementary questions.

- How will our opponents choose or be forced to counter our staple attack?
- How can we exploit the changes they make?

The more enterprising your answers to these questions, the more effectively your strategy will work. Simple repetition will not work, unless you have a significant advantage in power or pace.

Don't expect an overnight transformation when you have implemented a new strategy. Teams grow and develop over a number of seasons, through a process of player development and player recruitment. As soon as it's clear how you intend to play, you tend to attract players who enjoy that style of play. So it pays not to be narrowly constrained in your choice of strategy.

Initially, you're simply trying to change an emphasis within the existing team, and then by intensive practice to make some forms of attack seem natural. But it pays to have a vision of the rugby that you'll be playing in three years' time.

Your strategy is the foundation of consistent success, and the coach plans ahead to ensure its continuation and development from season to season. He must also plan how the team is going to exploit specific situations.

TACTICS

Tactics are your prepared team response to specific recurrent situations which you expect to encounter in every match or short sequence of matches. On p. 12 we look at the attacking and defensive responses to a typical situation: a scrum, attacking put-in, just outside the opposition 10m line, and 15m in from the attacking right touch. That is typical of the kind of situation it pays you to identify and prepare for. You ought to score from it, but you may not if your players don't recognise what's on and co-operate effectively to achieve it:

- *it's a tactical point* – one of those momentary pauses for kick-off (KO), drop-outs, scrum line-outs, rucks and mauls, penalties, fair catches. Such pauses allow you to launch a fresh co-ordinated attack;
- *at a particular point on the pitch* – an approximate distance from the goal-line, an approximate distance from touch;
- *which interests us because* – it's got a better than average chance of occurring and it's in a fairly critical area of the pitch;
- *the work we do on that scrum is representative* – we can apply it to any scrum 15–20m from the right touch, in a channel from the opposing 10m line to within a few metres of their line.

In *Total Rugby* I suggested a simple grid (see fig. 6) based on field markings, with an additional line 5m out from each goal-line and a further line down the middle of the field. Each intersection is a suitable point to consider as the locus of a situation – for example, a scrum, a ruck, a penalty. Start with the most critical ones, and work back into midfield.

Coach and players collaborate to work out:

 (i) how they are best equipped to attack from that point;
 (ii) which cues will indicate the most favourable form of attack;
(iii) what will need to be practised and by whom;
(iv) who decides and calls it.

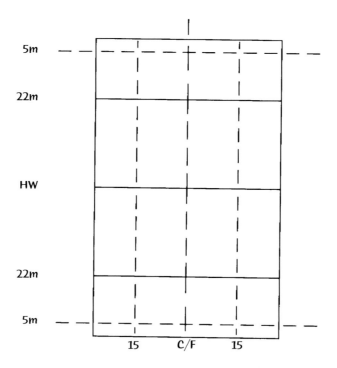

Fig. 6 **The tactical grid: representative situations**
The grid is merely a useful way of checking that you have answers for the
problems, and ways of exploiting the opportunities thrown up by tactical points
in the vicinity of the intersections. How is your team going to handle a scrum
on the opposing 22m line, at each of the three intersections? Thought about it?
You've had longer than your players will have, and you are sitting comfortably.

This has to be done completely realistically, in terms of the present abilities of
your present players. It may well direct the coach's attention to a need to improve
particular players' performance if he wishes to incorporate other attacks into the
repertoire; that must not affect present planning.

In deciding how to attack, coach and players may benefit from the following
considerations about tactical points:

THE MODEL

- At each, the effective, orthodox, defensive formation is utterly predictable – this
  makes it possible to plan attacks and also highlights any potential weakness
  due to bad positioning.

EXPECTATIONS

- At many of them, an opposing back may be left isolated and therefore easy to attack – typically a centre whose wing has dropped back to cover touch, or a fullback whose wings are up flat, or a blind-side wing;
- at some, a defending back may have been trapped, leaving a gap in his position, or, more likely, on the wing;
- at some, a stretched defence will be vulnerable to immediate continuation of the attack;
- at many, the attacking team can create space, clearing channels for attack by the positioning of its own backs;
- at most, provided you have approximate parity up front, you can control the release of the ball, and so:
  (a) control the tempo of play, so that you play at the pace that suits you;
  (b) control the amount of contact time in the forwards; and
  (c) create time to bring extra men effectively into attack.

FEEDBACK

- At each situation, your expectations will direct attention to two or three probable weaknesses; feedback from these will help you to select your immediate form of attack.

ACTION

Looking at situations in practices helps coach and players *see how best to deploy their existing repertoire*. Some forms of attack are far more effective in particular situations. The diagonal break to the right from a scrum by a scrum-half can be devastating from a 5m scrum on the opponents' line, but merely embarrassing to his own team in midfield; many tap penalties work only close to the line; one or two back-row moves are the same, and one or two ploys in the line-out.

It will also indicate *where the repertoire is inadequate*, and where everyone has to think about practicable additions. You need in each situation to face the possibility that the opposing pack is pressuring you. This will cut out various possibilities, and reduce the return on others. You need alternatives that don't depend on forward parity. At any single tactical point you want to limit the range of choice to the strategy and to two or three tactical ploys. This is in aid of speedy decision-making. Of course, this doesn't mean that your repertoire as a whole is so restricted: you want to maintain a balance between variety and thoroughly rehearsed slickness of execution.

Remember:

- possession is not assured – though in any match the probability becomes clear fairly quickly. Your scrum-half should always make clear as soon as he can whether or not we are getting the ball;
- time taken in holding the ball unnecessarily is time gifted to the defence – unnecessary delay always favours the defenders;
- any failure to act decisively or efficiently erodes or loses the potential initiative. You are doing not what you would choose to do, but what the opponents' pressure allows. Possession is only a potential advantage.

The second and third points emphasise the premium on speed. By the time coach and players have finished preparing a situation, they should have it reduced to simple elements which give a good speed/accuracy trade-off: a *model* of the situation including the opposition defence; *expectations* of where that defence will be weak, and of what cues will confirm its weakness; *scanning* with a sense of what our players are best equipped to do; leading to *action* selected from the prepared repertoire for that situation.

At this point you can see that we've prepared the way for committed, purposeful, co-ordinated action between team members – an acceptable definition of team play. We're no longer depending on the whim of whoever has the ball to dictate how we use it.

SUB-STRATEGIES

You'll have noted the need to predict how your opponents will try to counter your basic attack. Your players need advice on what to look for, and how to reply. Once again they need a model, expectations of what may happen, quick ways of checking, and immediate answers to the questions raised. In essence, as we've seen, the opposition (as single player or team) will tend to shift the emphasis of their defence: they'll commit more resources to checking the basic attack and fewer resources elsewhere. They buy strength at the cost of weakness, and it's at that weakness we intend to strike.

Often you can do it without greatly disrupting your basic pattern, by setting up simple ploys. For example, consistent attack in C3 invites a drift defence. If you draw a little diagram (see Fig. 7), you'll be able to see three consequent weaknesses: a weakness at stand-off; a potential weakness on the inside of each defender – who is being forced to cover more ground and run across; and a potential weakness in coverage of the area just behind the centres, which is usually covered by the defending back-row. You might suggest attack by the stand-off carrying the ball forward with inside-centre staying close and deep,

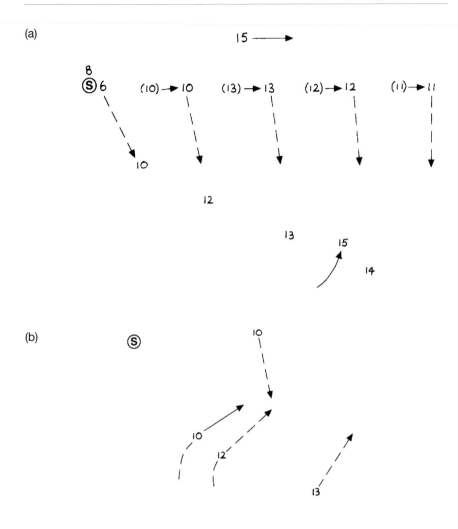

***Fig 7* Drift defence and one way of attacking it**
(a) Drift defence
(b) Basic reply
10 – a little slower
13 – a little wider
12 – a little deeper and closer

forcing the opposing stand-off into a 2 v 1, or you might suggest that any player under pressure aims to step back inside and feed supporting backs or forwards, or you might get your inside-centre doing little chips into the empty space. You might simply spin as normal to outside-centre with a miss, and he continues the staple attack in C3 or puts it back inside to inside-centre or stand-off depending on the state of the opposing defence. It depends to a great extent on the players you have and on their different abilities.

An alternative to these immediate solutions, however, is to set up a second staple activity; in effect, a *sub-strategy* concentrating attack in a channel whose defence has been weakened, in this case probably C1 or C3 on the blind-side. You can prepare for this with all the advantages that make the adoption of a main strategy so rewarding – clarity of purpose, clear coaching priorities, and a fresh sense of purpose in the players concerned. You can operate the complementary forms of attack economically since they'll often involve a different team unit.

You're aiming to set up a whole new set of problems for the defence; to create doubt in their mind and make it difficult for them to commit themselves to any single form of defence. If their back row have settled down happily to covering a wide attack, confident in what they are doing and setting off early and fast, it's very useful to have a whole set of attacks that initially exploit their early departure, and subsequently keep them concerned with C1.

What kind of sub-strategy you employ, how fully you develop it, and indeed whether you should have one at all, depends on the distribution of strengths in your team.

PURPOSEFUL BACK PLAY

Until coach and players recognise that the backs function best as a unit (as the forwards very obviously do in the scrum, and as the backs already do in defence), no individual back can be sure of getting the best chance to show what he can do. For that to happen, he has to get the ball in a favourable position, i.e. where he wants it, when he wants it, and running at the speed and in the direction he wants. We can arrange this consistently if we understand and apply central tactical control (see pp. 39 ff.), as well as basic rules on the use of space and time (see Part Four).

Of course it already happens in some fortunate teams. The Wallabies of the early eighties, for example; spinning the ball wide, turning up there in numbers, and playing it immaculately off the cuff. They could see where their strength lay, and turned it into a stylish and very effective strategy. Once they got it wide, excellent handling gave the ball to whichever player was running happily into space. There you have a back unit playing purposefully and employing a distinctive *strategy*.

Or consider how Gareth Edwards and J.J. Williams exploited that interesting situation – a scrum, on the left their put-in, 30m from the opposing line and 15m from touch. J.J. was given his chance because a central *tactical* purpose was at work.

In both cases you see not only purposeful, concerted play, but 'direction posts' for purposeful development: appropriate skills to be fostered; appropriate gambits; appropriate risk-levels; appropriate conditioning.

However, these are not the norm. All too often we're conscious of a lack of enterprise; of a disjointedness; of mechanical moves; of a failure to turn possession into points; of even talented teams depending on goal-kicking to put points on the board.

CENTRAL DECISION-MAKING

Our effort here is simply to show how we can encourage and accelerate enterprising concerted play in all teams, and make it accessible to less gifted players. We can develop co-ordinated forward play, co-ordinated back play and co-ordinated team play, focus it effectively, and even suggest precisely how to attack. We then have to decide who does the co-ordinating – who makes the necessary decisions.

One answer, very effective but limiting, is the coach. He can prescribe answers in surprising detail, provided he has adequate time with the team and provided the team accept his prescription. He can even get round that if he agrees the prescription after discussion. Consider this: 'From every line-out we'll move the ball to outside centre, with the fullback in. If we have an effective overlap, we'll play it; if not, outside-centre will kick down (but not into) the open touch. The aim is to force the opposing fullback to concede the throw-in.'

That is a typical prescription, indeed one that is actually practised in Japan, in whose games tradition coach-dominated play is culturally desirable. You can see its strengths:

- it allows concentration on a limited number of skills;

- there's not too much that can go wrong with it;

- it eliminates hesitation;

- the whole team knows what to expect, and can be drilled into effective response;

- the whole team feels confident in it.

You could take it a stage further: you could work out what the opposition will do to counter it, and what you will do in riposte. But, as a practice, it also has weaknesses:

- it doesn't promote decision-making or initiative among the players;

- the opposition know what you're going to do, so that it will rarely lead directly to a score – it works by attrition, and for that you need large supplies of ball;

- it may not develop a full range of skills in the player;
- it can be very dull.

At another level, heavily structured play can affect national teams: if the structures are reasonably similar in the best clubs (as they tend to be in New Zealand), it's an asset; if different (as in Japan), it's a problem.

On the whole, however, it's very successful in giving the players a purpose and the pleasure of making a direct contribution to a unified team performance. This approach marks a distinct advance on 'let's all do our own thing'.

Many of the UK's most successful teams have developed over the years an analogous unity of purpose by playing highly structured forms of rugby – almost always based on forward power. This is sometimes less coach dictated than player dictated: the traditional way of playing has brought success, which attracts players who enjoy that kind of rugby. You have a single, fairly clearly defined pattern of play, where the kinds of decisions to be taken are limited to a particular category of play – for example, how to get the ball back in front of the forwards.

Our present purpose is to combine the best of this kind of rugby – and specifically the strength of an underlying strategy – with greater variety of tactics; and to bring to our decisions greater flexibility, precision and opportunism. We're trying to devise a form of rugby and tactical control appropriate to the team that cannot expect to grind down its opponents, and must beat them by enterprise. For this we need decision-makers on the pitch who are able to respond to the opportunities and problems of the match as they arise.

The advantages of such tactical control have been recognised even in fluid games like basketball and soccer, in which possession can be channelled through a tactically gifted player who sets up the most appropriate form of attack. In a structured game, like American Football or rugby, the structure channels the ball to particular players at particularly critical moments, and those players exercise tactical control whether they wish to or not. In American Football, the quarter-back is the most prestigious player on the field, dictating very consciously how team possession is to be invested. In rugby, our halves exercise the same function but usually much less consciously: their tactical perceptiveness is rarely the first priority in their selection, and very little is done to improve it. Coaches, courses and books all preserve a discreet silence on the subject. If the halves aren't felt to be contributing enough tactically, the questions raised tend to be about selection rather than about coaching.

Consider their positional advantages for exercising tactical control:

- they handle the ball far more frequently than any other players;
- they receive the ball at the most critical moments in the game, when possession has just been won or retained, and in the most critical situations – the tactical points described above;

- they operate within at least a limited guarantee of space and time to assess the situation;
- they are centrally placed, ideal for fast communication;
- they can control the tempo of play.

And each of the halves enjoys more specific advantages.

THE SCRUM-HALF

- He is ideally placed to control attack (and defence) by the forwards: he has his head up, so he can see the channels into which forward-attack from tactical points is likely to be directed; he can see which are clear and which less well defended, which are wide and which narrow;
- he is close to the forwards, where he can judge accurately the balance of power between the packs, and so what is possible (in this match) in terms of forward attack or controlling the release of the ball;
- he is admirably placed to monitor and amend pack performance if he has models to apply and expectations of difficulties;
- he can communicate with everyone in the pack;
- he is the natural instigator and director of blind-side attack, which to be successful must be launched from as near the gainline as possible, whether by running or by kicking.

THE STAND-OFF

- He is close enough to get the ball while all the advantages of the tactical point are still operative, but he is under less pressure;
- he is better placed to scan the whole field;
- he is ideally placed to co-ordinate the play of the backs, by selection of striking point and mode of attack;
- in a team playing balanced rugby, he is best placed to co-ordinate team play.

Both have roles to play. In your team, which one is seen as the prime decision-maker may be determined by the balance of your strategy, by the actual situations under consideration, and the personalities of the two players.

As far as the coach is concerned, the question is clear: 'Given that the halves can't avoid decision-making on behalf of the team, and given that the quality of their decisions is a major factor in team success, do we try to make them more efficient or not?' And this leads, fairly inexorably, to the practical question: 'How do we do it?' Part Three, which follows, details advice on one way of doing it.

Part Three

Integrated tactical development

Stephen Larkham gets congratulated
Hardly a striking occasion in itself, but he was being congratulated for dropping a goal. England got knocked out of the World Cup by a Springbok who dropped five goals against them. What's really important is the cause of this rash of drop-kicks: it epitomises the difficulty of scoring tries against Rugby League-style extended defences. Australia won the World Cup, giving away one try in the process. In the previous editions of this book and *Total Rugby* it's been suggested that the pack should cultivate skills in running, handling and evasion, and drive forward into space rather than into serial rucks and mauls. In this edition I've tried to re-emphasise the desirability of developing this type of dynamic attack as a way of sucking in the forwards who can be spared from a slow moving ruck or maul to increase the coverage of the back defence, and make handling penetration more difficult than in the past. And, of course, such handling attacks can themselves lead to exciting scores. (Perhaps in Union, as in League, the value of the dropped goal should be reduced to a single point.)

3 **Making good choices**

The whole of this section is concerned with creating the right conditions for decision-making. Decision-making is the most characteristic element in games-playing, and the critical factor in maximising the return on our physical abilities and team possession. Yet it's the least developed aspect of coaching. We tend to work safely within the limits of our experience, and to concentrate on what we do most successfully. We teach techniques more effectively than skills, and skills more effectively than tactics. This is why forwards get a better deal from coaches than backs do, and why within forward-coaching there's disproportionately more emphasis on the mechanics of scrummaging than on the overall purposes of, say, running in the loose.

JUDGEMENT IN APPLYING INDIVIDUAL TECHNIQUE

As coaches, we can apply the general method described above to shape very effective techniques – techniques that won't let the player down. Once the technique is acquired, we can then devise forms of practice that give intensive repetition of the technique against appropriate degrees and forms of pressure, and do so economically in terms of space and time.

Properly administered, these should help the player groove the technique, so that it doesn't disintegrate under pressure, and accelerate his recognition of how it should be applied. Unfortunately, exercises of this kind aren't always properly administered. Too often the exercise is set up and the players left to get on with it; left to itself, intensive repetition can groove bad habits as easily as good. Such exercises should be seen as *coaching situations*, letting the coach see the player performing the technique far more frequently than in a match so that he can form opinions on how to help him in a matter of minutes rather than weeks. Once again, he'll be applying the general method: whichever technique is being practised, it will contain one or two elements which need to be monitored carefully.

The player's recognition of how the technique should be applied – its skilful application – also gets a chance to develop in the intensive repetition practice. As he faces the problem repeatedly he begins to work out, not always consciously, how to solve it. (We have ample experience of this; we do it in every aspect of our life.) And we don't *want* it to become a conscious concern; we shouldn't distract him with theory. The less we occupy his mind in dealing with the immediate micro-situation, the freer he is to concentrate on the developing team/game objective. Besides which, there's a limit to the scale on which advice will work. I don't know any 'advice' about the exact timing of a side-step. Recognising the context, yes: we can show the player how easy it is to side-step an opponent running flat and fast in defence. Setting up a practice that lets him choose between going straight for the line and side-stepping, yes: we can do it easily in grids. Technical advice about how to carry the shoulders, how to check, how to drive off, yes. But at a certain level this kind of advice is extremely hard to formulate and it is very doubtful whether it is of any help. It's far more effective to give the player a fair practical chance to develop the skill, so that he learns the limits within which he can operate and concentrates on working inside this range in the match.

JUDGEMENT IN COMBINED PLAY

This is a much easier level on which to intervene: we're working within time limits that allow rational analysis. I'm going to take a central example – a prime concern of every player, conspicuously absent from virtually all course programmes and represented in most books, if at all, by diagrams bearing little resemblance to the complexities of the game – judgement in support running. As coaches, we need to work out the *principles* involved, and devise ways of giving *intensive monitored practice* in implementing them.

I'm going to show how the basic method of investigation detailed in Part One will help us as coaches to simplify both the presentation of this to the players and the monitoring of their performance (as well as helping the players to monitor their own performance). We need a model based on principles, expectations about significant cues and problems, and advice on how to respond.

1. The first task is to make our players very aware of the need to control their positioning

In Chapter 7 of *Total Rugby* (pp. 121 ff.) I try to drive home the idea that every unopposed handling exercise is equally a support exercise; that the best pass is useless if the receiver is in a bad position. The coach must demand the same quality of performance in positioning as in handling.

The supporter needs a simple *criterion for being in the right position*. The best – because it has direct relevance to the game and it is totally simple – is that he should be in position to run on to a flat pass.

Second, he needs a simple *criterion for being there at the right time*. The best – because it has direct relevance to the game and is totally simple – is that the previous ball-carrier should never be forced to run with the ball, but be able to give a flat pass immediately. To clinch this there must be no doubt as to who the supporter should be: the players support in turn.

These simple conditions allow coach and player to judge performance. Is the player thinking far enough ahead to appear in the right position on time? We can increase the difficulty by stipulating, for example, how far away he should be; what direction he should be running in; how fast he should be running; and so on. Chapter 7 of *Total Rugby* (pp. 123 ff.) is full of such exercises, and the coach can invent more. Each one challenges the player to control his positioning by thinking ahead.

It may seem paradoxical, but it's only by imposing such conditions that we give the feedback that allows the player to assess his performance. Even then, we might be preparing the way for mechanical performance if we expected these exercises to be transported bodily into the match. But intensive handling exercises are designed precisely to give intensive repetition of particular techniques, and by their very nature are unsuited for direct incorporation into a match. They are designed to build up a variety of passing skills which can be applied by the individual to cope with the variety of situations in which he finds himself. And the positioning criteria are there for the same purpose – to encourage players to think ahead, decide where they need to be, and judge accurately how to get there so that they can cope with the wide variety of situations in which they find themselves.

Once you introduce the flat-pass rule into your handling practices, you'll never go back: it transforms idle wandering along into purposeful activity. To start every session with intensive, quality controlled handling is the best way of eliminating unforced errors when you're in possession, and an excellent way of warming up; it's also a basic way of improving the quality of support running throughout the team.

2. We can take this several stages further by introducing opposition

As soon as we do this, we bring in judgement of speed and distance in getting the pass away effectively, as well as an enhanced perception of what a good support position is. In effect, good timing of the pass means getting the ball away when it's too late for the defender to transfer his attention to the receiver, but before he's able to pressurise the ball-carrier. And good positioning, therefore, means:

- that the receiver is running into space;
- that he's far enough away from the ball-carrier to make the timing easy;
- but close enough to keep the technical problems of passing easy as well; and
- that he's up there ready to run onto a flat pass.

You'll find a detailed explanation of these points in the following pages. If you can explain these principles clearly, the players are again acquiring the criteria of successful positioning. Indeed, at this point you've created a model for them of what a 2 v 1 should be, and indicated the basic points ('expectations', 'cues') that they should check up on while carrying it out with good judgement.

We could develop this further by accustoming them to other combinations: for example, 3 v 2, with the two defenders conditioned to act in various ways (such as coming in one at a time; coming in together; standing; and advancing). In each case you are trying to develop principles of the 'unless you or your immediate supporter are running into space, pass the ball at once' variety; guidelines that simplify the problem for the player and that ideally are articulated by the players themselves.

3. We can begin to look directly at covering in the loose

The players have already got used to the idea that positioning is about working with other people, both to make their job easier and to give themselves the best chance of doing their own job well. We can expand that by putting them into support practices in which they're working over a bigger area with more people. Details of two of these can be found in *Total Rugby* pp. 302 ff. (following up a kick, and covering cross-field in defence), and these can easily be adapted to cover getting back behind a kick and covering cross-field in attack. In each case, I suggest that you set up the situation and simply let the players – all of them, not simply the forwards – have a go at it. With even very good teams, the result can reveal an embarrassing lack of overall model or awareness of particular possibilities. And yet, by suggesting principles and by drawing their attention to probabilities ('expectations'), you can transform their performance. What you've actually transformed is their grasp of precisely what they're trying together to do: you've given them a working model based on principles which they can apply to any support. For example, in following a kick:

- get your heads up and judge the landing point of the ball (establish the central axis of the operation);
- the first man can afford to try to pressurise the catcher by running straight towards the point, but must arrive in balance (limit opposition choices);
- subsequent runners are guided first by estimating where they can effectively get between the ball and their line (i.e. as far forward as they can without the risk of being outflanked); and then
- run off the players ahead of you to give *width* (and stop our being outflanked on either side), and *depth* (to catch the elusive runner).

These principles, understood, accelerate enormously the development of effective judgement in this phase of the game, especially when the players are offered intensive implementation of them in the suggested practices.

However, no matter how well designed the practice, the coach has to exercise quality control, bringing home as often as is needed the responsibilities of the individual player. To do this, he too must have his model clear, must have his expectations (both general and in terms of particular players), his priorities in checking them out, and be ready to intervene – ideally by stopping them in their tracks and asking them questions, or by bringing them together at the end of each run with specific comments.

4. We can start directing their attention to particular cues for action

It's quite likely that the exercises suggested above will mark the first time a coach has actively encouraged and helped the players to 'read the game'. Reading the game properly is like reading a book properly: it's a very purposeful attempt to see what the implications are for you. It doesn't depend on any particular visual acuity: input in the normal range is perfectly adequate to spot most cues. What matters is *directed* attention: you won't recognise cues unless you're looking for them, no matter how perfect your vision. You may 'see' them, but you won't see their significance; in the same way that you can 'read' a book yet totally fail to recognise what it means.

Again, the ability to read the game isn't an indication of a general awareness. It's a typical example of behaviour learned as a result of a particular interest. A keen bird-watcher will see birds where you see nothing; your wife will note dress details where you hardly register the dress. The keen rugby player who is alerted to the possibility will see and interpret give-away clues which the ordinary player misses completely.

In fact, there's nothing rare about the ability to do it in the game. It's just that some players employ it more spontaneously and consistently than others, and that doing it consistently tends to improve the ability. In many cases, the ability has simply never been activated: to suggest it, stimulate it by questions and praise its use is often enough to trigger it.

Praising its use is particularly important. Reading the game is useless if you don't act on what you detect: you've got to back your hunch. Initially, some of the hunches may be wrong, and it's at this time that the coach should think long term and give the player the support he needs. If the player is not prepared to make mistakes, he may end up making nothing. A further step in improving personal judgement in terms of support, therefore, is to *encourage the player's belief in his ability to pick up cues for action*, and to direct his attention to two sets of cues as follows.

Expectations within a given situation

If the team has effective communications, you may actually be told what, barring accidents, is planned in attack. If not, you should still have expectations based on practices and past matches of what we're likely to do in this situation, and, therefore, where you're most needed. You may have expectations of the same kind about a particular ball-carrier.

In defence, your starting point is intelligent guesswork about the opposition: what would I/we tend to do in this situation? what have they been doing in this situation? what have I heard they tend to do in this situation? what possibility must I cover because I'm here?

Give-away clues offered by other players

Every player benefits from a conscious effort to pick up as much information as possible from the players that directly concern him at that moment. Often your general cues from the situation will focus your attention on particular players, and they may offer, quite unconsciously, clues as to probable actions. Particular pairs of players are always engaged in this activity. The fullback, for example, is vitally concerned in the opposing stand-off, and to a lesser extent in the opposing fullback, and by them his observation may be switched to other players. The back row are very purposefully examining the halves, and, from their actions, other players. But everyone should cultivate it.

- *Positioning* – really look at his positioning; has it changed? is he getting ready to kick? making space for an extra man? getting ready to follow up a kick?

- *Attitude* – where's he looking? who's he looking at? who has he talked to? is anyone looking directly at him? is anyone out there changing position? is he taking pains not to look anywhere? is he signalling?

These various ways of encouraging intelligent running in the loose *work*: they help individual players to make intelligent decisions on how best to contribute to a team effort; and because they're based on principles they can be applied very flexibly to the full range of situations.

Yes, there's a limit to what enunciating principles can do. The method works best in a macro-situation where there's time to reckon out consciously what's likely to be effective. The kind of continuous cycle of assessment you'll find described below means that properly prepared or gifted players have time to apply it very frequently in the match, and especially in the time available at tactical points.

Evidently, the more completely we can incorporate the principles in practice situations the better: as far as possible we want to get beyond the need for conscious attention, so that the players we're working with act with the same apparent spontaneity as the very gifted player.

The same priorities are even more relevant in the personal micro-situation. We can offer advice on how to set up a situation, and walk through it so that it's very clear, but within that micro-situation there's a point where you must let the body think for you as it does for a child in the playground. You regain that spontaneity by giving the body plenty of practice – accustoming it to its role through intensive repetition.

GETTING BETTER JUDGEMENT AT THE BREAKDOWN

If we proceed as suggested in the last section, it's comparatively easy to improve the support running of our players. But another set of problems face them when they arrive, typically, at a breakdown with the ball on the deck.

The first thing to do is to give them the maximum opportunity to set up their arrival properly. For example, it's always more effective to arrive running fairly straight rather than across; in balance rather than committed to a straight line; with time to look rather than in a blind panic. The key is speed: speed of response so that they're two or three metres on their way from the tactical point before the opponents react; speed of acceleration (those first few steps are extremely important); speed of running (we've got to condition them to repeated high-speed efforts); accuracy of line, based on constant response to feedback.

Even so, they'll often be faced with a complex situation – bodies on the deck, opponents arriving, the ball bobbing around – and a very limited opportunity to assess what to do. And the added pressure of knowing that retaining or regaining possession in this situation correlates highly with team success. What they need is to have the situation simplified; to have a list of priorities; to know the cues for action; and to have all things integrated in experience rather than as intellectual concepts.

This is not the kind of task that coaches have commonly tackled: it's a lot easier to stick to scrummaging. My own first attempt was very simple. It took the form of a cyclic exercise – an exercise so structured that it automatically repeats giving more or less intensive repetition of a desired situation. It consisted basically of a single file of five players, trotting one behind the other down a line.

Player 1, with the ball, accelerated, put the ball on the ground, and turned as defender. Player 2 was faced with the decision – was player 1 far enough back to let him pick up and drive, or ought 2 simply to fall and secure the ball for 3, 4 and 5 to ruck over?

I was prompted to elaborate this by the analysis Brian Ashton brought back from the England tour to New Zealand in 1985. He talked about and demonstrated an exercise much used in New Zealand to help players cope more effectively with the situation. Using some of the categories he described, the following exercise emerged.

Practice one

5 4 3 2 1*. . . . . *. 1

All five players are trotting down a line – say the 22, since this will keep them close to the coach. Player 1 has the ball*. He accelerates out in front, puts the ball down, and turns to act as defender.

How many strides he takes before turning can be controlled by the coach, who can create the different situations outlined below. So too can the degree of commitment he offers in defence, but we need him to build up opposition as soon as the basic pattern of the exercise is established. Eventually, we want an open confrontation: it's just as important that he learns what to do in defence as well as attack.

The numbers taking part ensure that each of the players will experience all the roles involved over five repetitions and the exercise is cyclic: it will go on till the coach stops it.

As player 1 turns to defend, *player 2* has a choice of actions.

1. The coach *limits* the choices – he offers four;
2. he puts them *in order of desirability*;
3. he provides *intensive practice* within the cyclic exercise, controlling how much space is left between defender and ball and moving towards a random placement.

First choice: Can I pick it up and drive forward?
Coaching advice: check the space, check freshness and skill, check that the ball is stationary and dry. (How much space/time he needs will be established in the exercise.)

Second choice: Should I fall, secure, and try to get up and drive forward?
Coaching advice: (you've decided against trying the pick-up) yes, especially if you're not sure of fast support.

Third choice: Should I fall, secure, and roll to feed?
Coaching advice: (you doubt if you've time to get back on your feet) yes, if it's on – if the ball is dry and the support available.

Fourth choice: Should I fall, secure, and let 3, 4 and 5 ruck over?
Coaching advice: (you haven't time to roll and feed) yes, we must control that ball.

In the match, this situation might be faced by any of the forwards, but most often by an open-side flanker, one of whose principal roles is securing that loose ball ('If it's on the deck, it's mine.').

As player 2 goes in for the ball, *players 3, 4 and 5* are faced with a choice: what should I do given:

The space he's got?
Coaching advice: in your first- and second-choice actions, you want him to

support from deep, controlling his speed to let him accelerate on to the ball. Don't overrun him as he checks to pick up, or fall and pick up. If they're on, check early then accelerate in support. In your third-choice action he'll have less space, but there's no likelihood of a ruck: check, and show him your hands. In your fourth choice, there's no space, and the ruck is inevitable – aim to get under your opponent with your hips below your shoulders, and lift him up and back. You may have to start with your knees on the deck.

The conditions?
Coaching advice: bad conditions will inhibit the player in front of you; he'll probably try the second choice instead of the first, and the fourth rather than the third.

The player he is?
Coaching advice: you're practising with him – get to know what he likes, what he prefers to do.

As the first cycle ends, there'll be a supporter running into space (choices one, two, and three) or a player picking up at the back of the mini-ruck. He runs forward slowly, far enough to let the rest get back on their feet; puts the ball down; turns to act as defender – and the whole cycle has started again.

Coaching points
- Control the ball-carrier by prescribing a number of steps/degree of active opposition, until it's grooved; then open it up.
- If you want more opposition, depute a sixth player to accompany the ball-carrier each set of cycles – he simply drops back time after time in defence.
- Watch one player at a time.
- You can build up the number of players, but the point of starting with 5 is that it gives the maximum activity and the maximum range of roles.
- It's tiring. This can be an excellent form of heavy conditioning: it satisfies the basic requirement of high work-rate ('Do it – and run.'); but until the form is grooved, fatigue may simply lead to sloppiness.
- If the cyclic shape proves difficult, re-jig it as in the following diagram.

Practice two

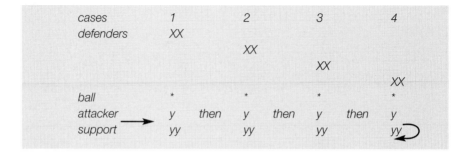

cases	1		2		3		4
defenders	XX						
			XX				
					XX		
							XX
ball	*		*		*		*
attacker	y	then	y	then	y	then	y
support	yy		yy		yy		yy

You can work this very easily. Put markers down as a guide to where the players can start from in the four cases. The diagram is quite accurate in relative positions, but players with particular speed off the mark may distort it.

Practice three

To establish a fast, accurate, efficient action, you can use either of the coaching situations we've just looked at. Once you're happy with the options and their execution, you can concentrate on contact with the opposition. This creates a sequence very likely to occur in the match, and ensures that the player maintains concentration.

Case 1: the player picks up with space ahead of him
We're looking to create a 2 v 1. Urge the player with the ball to run for the edge of the defenders, and for his supporters to work on getting into space outside him.

Case 2: the player picks up with very limited space ahead of him
We want to go forward, but we must protect the ball. We want him to beat a man if possible; each metre he goes forward makes it easier to attack, harder to defend. Encourage him to think that he can 'always' beat a man. He doesn't need to swerve or side-step, though the talent may well be there: he can step inside, roll off, or whatever else occurs to him. Sheer determination may count for as much as skill. The basic idea is 'run for space', with as little deviation from straight down the pitch as possible.

As soon as he knows he's liable to be checked, his main aim becomes not to go forward but to protect the ball. He's the man responsible for getting the ball back. If it doesn't come back, it's long odds he'll let the opposition get its hands on it. So he must choose how to make contact. The two clearest ways are described fully in *Total Rugby* pp. 147 ff.: power step and turn where you have space enough to do it: drive in, with shoulder blades level with hips, spine pointing straight up the pitch and the ball back at the thighs, held in both hands, if you haven't. The practices described there can groove these actions, so that they can be taken with minimum delay.

If he's tackled from the side or behind, he should try to get the ball down, where the first supporter can pick up and drive forward in turn. The best preparation for this is another cyclic exercise – see pp. 53 ff. of *Total Rugby*. If all else is impossible, he's got to fight to get the ball down behind him when he hits the ground.

Case 3: the player falls, rolls, and feeds

All supporting players, in all situations, need to look ahead and gauge the best speed of approach. Start fast, arrive in balance: that's still the best advice. The slight check as the player ahead falls and rolls may see you sail in front of him if you haven't judged your arrival. Ideally, you want to accelerate through the ball.

Unless the supporters are well back, it's best for the ball-carrier to lob it up in front of them, so that there's a margin while the ball is in the air.

Once the supporters have it, they'll be looking for first- or second-choice action.

Case 4: the player dives in to secure the ball on the ground, and the rest ruck over him

The supporters 3 and 4 have the critical job in creating an effective ruck. Their job is to roll the opposition back over the ball and expose it. To do this, they need to get in just under the opposing player's centre of gravity, with their hips lower than their shoulders, and lift the opposing mass back and up. To do this they may have to start with their knees on the ground. It's unlikely that they'll arrive together, though you do your damnedest to make sure they do: the single greatest advantage of the All Blacks is their superior fitness, their ability to keep galloping round the paddock under a single blanket. If you arrive 'firstest with the mostest', you're going to win the ball. If you can't, it pays to be very efficient. If you can convince your players of the need to concentrate on a tight, narrow, dynamic wedge – 'in, lift, forward' – and get them to keep their eyes wide open and go in intelligently, it pays off.

If your ball-carrier is on his feet, the first supporter should bind with him, preferably with the ball between them. If not, he acts as marker and aims to get beyond the ball, and the third supporter joins with him: we need two players bound together as the front row of our ruck. By setting out these priorities, we give the players a chance to exercise judgement. If they don't understand the principles, they can't judge effectively and consistently.

We then want the next three going in to form a second row. A No. 8 and two flankers, as it were. Of course, it may not be easy, may not be possible – but the more clearly they understand that aim, the more frequently they'll manage it. And they've got to have one clear imperative before them: to keep moving relative to the ball, which means to look for that ball. They drive forward over it – that's the ideal, since it guarantees the opposition will be off-balance in defence – or they steer (not boot) it back. The last man controls it, like a No. 8 in the tight, till the scrum-half calls for it. Which may be immediately it's available. Once again, what's needed is an understanding of principle.

Later we can move on to defence. That's equally important. It's futile trying to push against a tight dynamic ruck: you've got to collapse the front of it before it really gets formed; while it's still so small the referee lets you do it. Drive in low at the front with enough players to check it, and cover the sides. Once you've got the whole show on the road, each put-down of the ball leads to a genuine confrontation.

There's nothing in the least theoretical about the practices – the theory is in setting them up to promote particular mental processes which games players need, and very good games players are blessed with. But to have a maximum practical effect they need to be used by the coach as coaching situations. They will have an effect, left to themselves, but it may not be good. The great opportunity they offer is for the coach to see, as often as necessary, one player or group of players coping with this important situation, so that he can assess their performance and then intervene to improve it. Coaching *is* intervention.

4 Improving tactical decisions

Improving tactical decision-making – how the team is to use the ball from tactical points – is a natural development of coaching expertise. It is no different in kind from the examples of improving judgement individually or as part of a team effort that we have already looked at. Indeed, in some ways it's easier: it corresponds more closely to running in the loose in that it can be rationally handled, within manageable time limits and without total dependence at particular moments on innate abilities.

In essence, it means giving conscious control of how we use the ball to centrally placed players, providing them with:

- models of recurrent situations;
- expectations of where there will be defensive weaknesses; plus
- actions planned and practised to allow effective strikes.

In all of this, it's counter-productive to treat them in isolation. They're best seen as typical players with special responsibilities: the qualities we want in them are qualities of value in every player, but we have to give them more concentrated attention. Equally, they ought to feel that they're operating consensus policies which the whole team have helped to shape, and which the whole team have been prepared to put into practice. The coach will play a very important part in shaping these policies and in winning the team's trust in them, and then in the detailed preparation of how they are to be implemented.

Seeing the preparation of tactical decision-making as a team concern also simplifies the coach's task. No coach can devote a great deal of time to a single player or a single aspect of play, and this integrated approach makes the whole thing workable. It also encourages a fast response to any call made, by players who have been fully involved in the setting up of tactical plans.

This chapter offers detailed advice on how to set up a programme of tactical preparation, and how to cope with the problems that appear. But it's much more than this, since it deals with tactical development and team development as a single integrated process, and the problems it covers are common to all players to some degree. Moveover, much of it applies to you as coach, selector and referee, as well as to the players.

RISK-TAKING AND THE TDM

The core of judgement is accurate risk-assessment. In essence, we have to weigh possible gains against possible losses. We don't mechanically go for minimum risk; we don't push risk-taking to extremes: we use our personal and tactical resources intelligently.

Even when choosing from a limited repertoire of team options, the TDM is involved in risk-taking on a comparatively large scale. His errors tend to be far more costly than those of the individual player making personal decisions. This can be inhibiting: the player may need support from the coach, especially when things go wrong. It helps if the TDM recognises four categories of risk.

That's an acceptable risk . . .

The whole of team preparation should build up an accurate sense of your standard of acceptable risk. If, for example, you've identified and practised the situations that make it easy to attack from your 22 (see figs 8 and 9), given your level of basic skills, such a risk is acceptable.

That's a risk we needn't take . . .

The fact that we *can* attack from our 22, given the right situation, doesn't mean that we *should* do so now, at this particular moment, in this particular match. But if your TDM consistently underestimates your team capacity, and fails to employ their range of options, you need to find out why. It may be that the players aren't happy with the options; it may be that you need another TDM.

That's a risk we must take . . .

There are moments when you *must* seize the initiative – when time or the opposition's momentum are against you. The sooner you recognise the danger, the less risk you need run: you act decisively on the first reasonable chance that offers itself. If you wait until the situation becomes desperate, you may have to take desperate risks.

That's too much of a risk . . .

No matter how well-prepared the team may be, there are times when your options are severely restricted. It does team morale no good at all for the TDM to prove that some things are impossible even for them. Backing a long shot usually makes a bad situation worse.

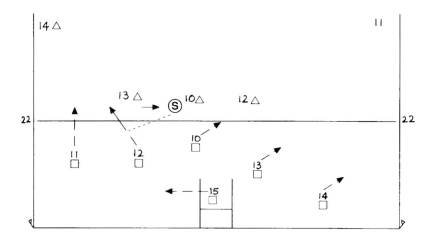

***Fig. 8* Attacking an isolated defender (1)**
The kind of situation in which the opposition's expectations can open the way
for attack. All your backs should be able to function efficiently as stand-offs. The
cue is the depth of opposition 14.

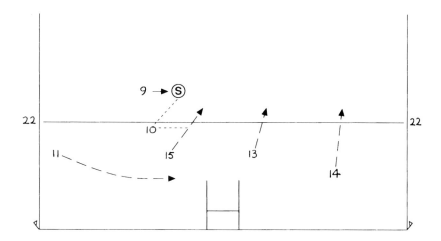

***Fig. 9* Attacking an isolated defender (2)**
The kind of start in which the ball crosses over behind the scrum often runs
into problems because the switch is made a little too quickly. If 10 holds it just a
little longer, so that he gives the time to let opposing 6, 7 and 9 register his
'indecision', and pulls them in, he'll create space for 15.

And the same 'indecision' may open up the blind-side as Ollie Campbell's did
against Scotland in 1984.

As readers of *Total Rugby* will know, I favour high-skill/high-risk rugby as the most memorable form of the game for all concerned. On purely utilitarian grounds, however, any team that cannot be sure of winning its fair share of possessions *must* build the high-skill/high-risk factor into its team preparation: without it, they may not be able to win at all.

Acceptable risk levels are a very clear indication of coaching attitudes and abilities. The team that is coached well with high quality-control standards can operate at what for a less well coached team would be quite unacceptable levels of risk. Every time a coach fails to demand high standards, in whatever aspect of rugby he's coaching, he reduces the whole team's ability to exploit opportunities. In the end, it always comes down to the individual player, and how well he has been prepared to play his part in the team. It's never a 'team' that makes mistakes, it's always an individual player who happens to be playing in that team. The good coach accepts that as his starting point in all that he does: he constantly intervenes to improve individual performance, and through doing that he improves unit and team performance. And it's that high level of individual competence that permits the team to play exciting rugby.

ESTABLISHING A PROCEDURE

The single immediate step you take with your potential TDM is to insist that he calls. Starting with pre-set routines – programmed unopposed and sequences, for example – he has to make the call, early and loud. In unopposed, the coach trots along behind him demanding the call. Every time unit or team practise together formally, he's making calls, directing operations.

Once this is established, you wait for bad ball to reach him. You explain that:

- he never proceeds with the call if things are going wrong – he never passes the buck;
- he must be ready to simplify play – usually, he'll find, by kicking – without surrendering the initiative;
- he must have a simpler, but still effective, alternative in mind. In essence, he has to ask: 'If I have to kick the ball, where should I put it?'

You can see that by this time we've three steps:

1. a provisional decision (what he'll do if things work out);
2. communication (he calls to the others);
3. a provisional alternative (what he'll do if things don't work out).

You needn't elaborate this to the player. You needn't present it to him as a process; that might merely distract him. You simply require him to make the call and have an alternative worked out if it goes wrong. He has a job to do, and that's the basis of it.

That job is to make things happen. Above all, he must not let events control him. He must control and order events in the best interest of the team. You'll probably be reinforcing and reorganising what he already does in a limited way.

MODELLING THE PROCESS

If you make him conscious of the workings of his mind, it will inhibit his performance. It will have much the same effect as trying to get a player to swerve by giving him precise instructions about his feet. The whole strength of both decision-making and swerving is that they're there already, like Michelangelo's statues in the marble, waiting to be revealed. You're trying to establish the process actively, in practice, on the field.

You, however, already have a fairly clear idea of the process. It's going to be another application of the basic approach we've been considering: model, expectations, scanning, response. As each situation (model) develops, he has certain expectations of where the team can attack, and he's checking a very small number of cues that will guide him to an effective response. We're going to try to simplify and accelerate this by showing him what to look for, and how the team is best equipped to exploit it. As always, we'll show him primarily by doing it, so that the team learns at the same time as he does.

I've kept you thinking of a single player as TDM. Often one player will emerge as naturally qualified to lead. Sometimes the character of your team and strategy will dictate that one player should lead. But the points made already on pp. 61 ff. above suggest that there's a very strong case for thinking of your halves as a tactical unit, each responsible for certain facets of attack. If you adopt this, then you treat them always as a unit, talking and demonstrating to them as a pair, so that as a pair they come to recognise the situations in which one or other should have primacy. Where there are disagreements in practices or matches, you talk it out, making each occasion a chance to clarify what's best for the team. One great advantage of this is that you'll rarely lose them simultaneously: there'll be someone there to lead.

I'm going to continue writing of the TDM as a single player: you interpret as you wish.

TIME LIMITS

It's clear that the amount of time available to us for making a decision is limited, and that we must try to reduce our need as much as we can. The less time we take to make the decision and communicate it, the less time we give our opponents to regroup. Delay favours the defenders. So we need a fast call, with the ball available to be played as soon as possible.

The simplest way of accelerating the call is to reduce the options. We need a varied repertoire, but at any tactical point it benefits the TDM to have a very limited number of relevant calls to make. This is one of the great benefits of thinking in terms of 'situations'.

But we don't want to be rushed: we mustn't try to play the game at a tempo higher that we can efficiently cope with. Within reason, we can control the tempo, and the time available for making and communicating decisions, by controlling the release of the ball by the forwards. They release the ball immediately the scrum-half calls for it, and only when he calls for it. But how long they can hold it depends on opposition pressure: it's futile to ask them to hold it at a massive cost in terms of energy and morale.

So how are we to ensure a consistently fast yet accurate call? The only way is for the TDM to be consistently ahead of play. This allows him to judge without immediate pressure, and call in time for the other players to rehearse their roles. But to do this he has to be constantly switched on, constantly attentive. How can we improve his concentration?

RAISING THE ATTENTION LEVEL

Here is a 12-point programme for raising the attention level of every player in the team, and especially that of the TDM. It's directed at him, but it would be far less effective if he benefited from it in isolation: the more alert the team is, the faster it will respond to his calling, or to opposition threats.

1. The most effective way of focusing attention is to convince the player that we expect him to do a job, and that the job demands it. As soon as he has a particular personal interest, and he knows he's going to be judged on it, he sits up and takes notice.

2. We emphasise the value of mental rehearsal: 'It's a scrum, our put-in, on the right, 20m out from their line, 15m from touch . . . what do I check on? What can we do?' This is a way of stimulating interest, and of general 'psyching up' common in all forms of sport.

3. We keep asking him the same kind of question in practices.

4. We can extend it to problem-solving on behalf of the team: 'What do we do if they play a drift defence against us at line-outs?'

5. We can involve him in coaching other players, both technically and tactically, which will force him to look for the significant, and articulate it.

6. We can encourage him, as part of his responsibility for the unit, to analyse its performance each run and to put things right.

7. We can give him a special focus, which is an excellent way of activating attention: in all practices we link what we're doing as a team to the relevant cues ('scrum-half will take it blind because their winger is lying back . . . if he were up, we could chip into the box . . .').

8. We can involve him in the selection of team tactics right from the start, and encourage him to pick out the cues of positioning, isolation and space (see Part Three).

9. We can play extended 'predictive unopposed' (see page 87) with the TDM calling not only the tactics but all the tactical points, so that he is forced to concentrate on the emerging situation and probable developments.

And we can screen out some of the distractions that get in the way of concentrated attention.

10. We can create intense pressure situations in practice. One source of inattention is opposition pressure: think of the stand-off behind our line receiving the ball with the opposing back row in close pursuit. If we can spot particular weaknesses we can set up appropriate practices. In this case, you'd put the scrum-half with half-a-dozen balls about 10m out, with two or three 'opponents' just behind him. They follow in, singly then in pairs, to harass the stand-off. The scrum-half controls the tempo, which gradually mounts. The stand-off has targets for each kick. Incidentally, this should be a practice for everyone taking part: each one has something to learn.

11. We can control the nature of his environment just before we go out. The TDM, like most players, should go out calm and assured: over-arousal, and consequent anxiety, can destroy his concentration (see page 74).

12. We can tighten up reactions to the referee's whistle. As soon as the whistle goes, the ball is dead; and so, for some players, is concentration. They turn round, for example, and trudge back. They stop concentrating and for that moment are vulnerable.

These are basically technical answers to inattention at a technical level. For many players, they are all you will need. However, there's another category of distraction which is much more difficult to handle.

At its best, concentration empties the mind of all extraneous factors: the very good player is able to focus on game objectives throughout the match, undistracted by pain, fatigue or emotional involvement. He is enormously committed in terms of nervous resources, but once on the pitch he is detached in emotional terms, scarcely aware of his opponents as people, concerned only with implementing game priorities. He is insulated from distractions like crowd noise: he may become aware of it only when he can't communicate with the player standing a metre in front of him. He is insulated to a considerable extent from discomfort and fatigue: he goes on concentrating even when his body may no longer be able to make an appropriate response; he is unconscious of self; he is dispassionate.

There's a no-doubt apocryphal story of an American tennis coach who placed a ball in front of a player and challenged him to concentrate on it for four minutes. When the player's eyes flickered, the coach said: 'Bjorn can do that for four hours.' Apocryphal or not, accurate or not (for like any other bodily function, attention will vary in intensity over, say, 80 minutes), that contains a truth. What doesn't come over is that Bjorn, on song, didn't have to try, didn't distract himself by telling himself to concentrate. He was totally absorbed in the doing. Of course, when he is not on song, that concentration can be fragmented. And equally, he doesn't have to make a great effort to insulate himself from his opponents, or from the state of the match.

What can the coach do to promote a state of constant attention in his players?

- He can encourage the player never to think in terms of winning or losing. To think about the result is simply to distract the mind without purpose: complete concentration on the 'now' is the only way to influence the result positively; and the only match result that personally affects the player is his personal commitment to doing his best. That sounds like, and may well be, philosophical advice, but it is offered as the technical truth: you don't win by thinking about winning, but by concentrating on making your finest contribution at this particular moment in the match, whether it's the first or the last.

- He can encourage the players never to be aware of themselves as subjects of spectator interest. If a player needs an audience he should recognise that the only important audience is the team and the coach, and the way to impress them is by judgement and commitment. If he doesn't satisfy them, he may lose his place, and with it the attention of the spectators at large.

  This need to be a centre of attention often goes back to personal insecurity. Many players use the game to provide an imagery of self; some to provide a crutch for a sense of inadequacy. They may react fiercely to criticism, as if it were criticism of 'them'; they react badly to injury; they are generally difficult. No coach welcomes such a player, because he absorbs too much time and energy, but there's little doubt what the most effective treatment is: welcome him as a person rather than a player; encourage him to think well of himself as a person rather than as a player. It isn't easy.

- The player who makes a mistake, and spends the next few seconds 'regretting' it, or, worse still, the player who suffers from someone else's mistakes and spends the next few seconds regretting it, has lost concentration. He is a typical case of this general category of distraction: he is thinking not about the game, but about himself. The coach must encourage him to focus on the immediate game objective – usually, in this case, tidying up the mistake.

If we can reach a state of constant attention (and remember, every step towards it is worthwhile), then we can be sure that the tactical cycle of attention is a real possibility. All this means is that the process repeats itself again and again throughout the match: the very good player 'never' stops forecasting, scanning, backing his hunches. (In the case of the TDM, you should recognise that as soon as the implementation of his tactical call has started, the cycle starts again *on a personal level*: he's predicting whether he can get back into the action in this phase of play, and if so where and how. It's only when the chance of this has receded that he switches to a tactical mode, and the process of preparing the next call begins. See fig. 10)

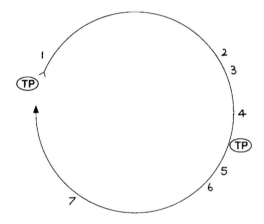

Fig. 10 **The recurring tactical cycle**
1. After the TP the TDM switches to personal decision-making: how can he contribute to the tactical purpose?
2. As the next TP approaches – for example, he can predict a tackle – he begins to model the situation.
3. Properly prepared, he has clear expectations of what may be on.
4. He starts looking for the cues that he, the coach, and the team have noted as significant.
5. He makes the appropriate call, clear and loud, and as early as he can.
6. He decides on a provisional alternative in case he gets bad ball.
7. It's 'GO', which he doesn't call, or 'CHANGE', which he will call.
1. After the TP . . .

STRESS CONTROL MECHANISMS

We can also help to make sure that they prepare for the match effectively. Some of the most highly motivated players approach major events – and in some cases ordinary matches – in a spirit of commitment with which ordinary players may not be familiar. The process of mental and emotional preparation may last several days, fuelled by mental rehearsal of the match to come.

In such cases, the danger is not of under-arousal – the target of those changing-room tirades which do so little to fulfil their purpose – but of over-arousal, and consequent anxiety. This anxiety can undermine the preparation for the match.

To control these contrary impulses, most good players use a variety of practical methods.

Ritual

There is a great deal of comfort to be found in established patterns of behaviour. Most players approach a big match within a behaviour pattern that they know works: the distribution of conditioning effort and rest, of rehearsal and distraction, of excitement and calm is one that they have cultivated. This large pattern has room within it for smaller rituals, right down to which boot is put on first, how the socks are held up, and how the last moments are spent before going out.

Relaxation methods

Volumes have been written about different methods of relaxation. One I found of great value was controlled breathing exercises. I wasn't wholly conscious of it as a relaxation exercise; I thought it was a way to improve my lung capacity. It involved controlling breathing in, holding it, and breathing out in a timed cycle, starting at 15 seconds for each element and aiming at 60 seconds. It's evident now that whatever it did for my physical condition, it certainly was a way of reducing stress.

Mantras

Many athletes use a mantra as a calming device. It's possible to see this simply as a detail in the governing ritual, but it seems to merit special mention. Throughout my playing career I found calm in Isaiah 40.31: 'They that wait upon the Lord will renew their strength; they will mount up on wings like eagles; they shall run and not be weary; they shall walk and not faint.'

The best use and adaptation of these methods for individual players has to be found by experiment, and may differ from one player to another. But the broad categories probably hold good.

The state of mind that most characterises the good player actually involved in the game is serenity: he is totally involved in the game as another might be in reading a book, or turning a pot. The serenity comes from detachment; a forgetting of the personal and the petty. And this impersonality is matched by a dispassionate attitude to the opponent. The very good player simply has no time, far less a taste, for personal vendettas: he is governed by games objectives, not personal ones.

This serenity is found even in training. The sheer quantity and quality of conditioning work undertaken by a top player is daunting: he ends each session exhausted. But his serenity is not affected: going out for the next session is easy. The work undertaken in training and the efforts made in the match are natural, without emotional strain.

In the match, he remains cool, even detached. At the bottom of a pile-up he is still figuring what the opposition will do next. Nothing surprises him: he simply responds to it immediately. Emotion merely clouds that response. Because he is so responsive he appears constantly to be ahead of play, picking up tiny cues and interpreting them in such a way as always to be at some advantage. To him it seems easy and natural.

Although this may seem far from the experience of typical players, I'm sure it's a difference in degree rather than in kind, and that if any player sets out to activate such responses they'll flnd they can do it. Like prediction and decision-making, for which it's the ideal base, it improves with practice.

This state of mind is by no means confined to games players. I've heard it exactly matched by RAF fighter pilots and seen it described in books on bushido. This suggests that it may not be an uncommon state given an appropriate situation.

Evidently, it's worthwhile having every player consider these ideas, which come perhaps as a fairly radical alternative to existing stereotypes of the rugby player's state of mind. It seems especially relevant, however, to the TDM, whose need for mental clarity and speed of response is even greater than that of the rest of the team.

5 **Eight steps to tactical efficiency**

Tactical efficiency is measured by how seldom we waste possession; how seldom we commit ourselves to attacks that were never on. To make it a practical reality we need unit and team exercises that will give us:

- a well-rehearsed repertoire of attacks to choose from – our players must feel confident and at ease in each element so that they respond fast and with insight to the call;
- for each representative situation, two or three appropriate attacks – with a clear identification of the cues for choice;
- effective sequencing of attack – to create a sense of continuity in our play, and derive maximum benefit from the previous phase;
- speedy tactical calling – to maximise our advantage (we won't always go straight into an attack, but we need to be able to);
- identification of defensive counters to our staple and appropriate ways of exploiting them – if our staple forces a form of defence on the opposition, we must be able to spot it, and exploit its weaknesses by practised means.

If we can put together a programme of team and TDM preparation that will improve our abilities in the above five respects, we'll have the makings of an outstanding team performance. And if to that we can add:

- scanning for opportunities by the TDM – to let us take advantage of a positional or technical inefficiency in the opposition that doesn't normally present itself

that will be the icing on the cake.

Everything that's written below assumes that quality standards have already been established in the basics, and that it's a priority of both coach and player that these standards should be maintained. Of all the basics, the two most important to enterprising attack are handling and positioning. Time spent working on quality in both, internalising a pride in achievement, and polishing the skill is time well spent. It needs detailed application. But it pays off in expanding the whole range of possibilities, and reducing what in other teams might be unacceptable risks to an acceptable level. Never let the players – yourself, if you're a player – be sloppy in handling; never allow them to practise weaknesses. From the very start of practice, it's got to be quality, quality, quality. Fortunately, handling and positioning are two of the easiest skills for the player to monitor and analyse for himself: encourage him to do so. Now to the eight steps of the chapter title.

1. ESTABLISH EACH BASIC START WITHIN THE UNIT

We're looking to create a limited repertoire in which the players have complete confidence, and from which the TDM can select an option easily and with commitment.

It's convenient to think of each tactical decision as being a 'start' – a gambit. It focuses attention on the need for the players concerned to create an advantage. Be prepared to improvise and work hard to capitalise on it. The most important start is your basic, strategic staple, and it needs to be worked on intensively. Whenever there's no cue in a particular situation, this is what you'll tend to do, because it's the thing you do best. In addition, you need a variety of other starts, with the same aim of creating an advantage for one player, and the same responsibility of working hard and intelligently to capitalise on it.

Every start needs to be used with judgement to bring pressure on one particular weakness; and it has to be applied with judgement of timing and space.

You need to establish it by a process of guided trial and error, running through it, thinking, talking, changing. And then you must polish, polish, polish. Most starts that fail – 90% of them – do so because they haven't been adequately prepared.

i. The most effective start positions

Most of your starts will call for some adjustment of positioning. In an ideal world your players would subtly shift into these positions on the move, completely concealing their changed intentions. In the real world, it's a better bet to change initial positions for different purposes. You'll find this fully covered in Part Four. However, you may find it useful now to think of three categories:

1. local shifts to allow a particular interchange – for example, a player moving a little wider and deeper to let him come through straight on a switch, instead of being forced to choose between running slowly or being forced back in;

2. creating space to allow certain kinds of attack – for example, moving your front three to the left of a scrum to open up a channel for back-row attack on the right, or vice-versa;

3. special formations for special events (see for example, page 67).

ii. Timing (1)

The signal from the scrum-half that the ball is available, and that preliminary movement – including the movement looked at above – can take place (see page 116). Of course, this may not be necessary, and the scrum-half will go straight to . . .

iii. Timing (2)

The moment when the scrum-half calls for and receives the ball. This is the standard starting time for the normal attack.

iv. Angles of run

If your work on intensive handling and positioning has begun to pay off, the players should have a sound grasp of principle about angles of run. However, you can reinforce it in the particular context. It may be as simple as ensuring that a player isn't going to block his pass by running too straight, or that a winger comes back in slightly to preserve space outside him.

v. Your own expectations of potential problems and solutions

You will practise these starts frequently, with our present players and probable reserves. To do this quickly and effectively you need to clarify your model and establish the points on which to concentrate: those most likely to give trouble. It's these you'll focus on in the first setting up of the start, explaining as you go what the problems are and how to avoid them, and again in monitoring performance. In your own learning phases, however, you learn by setting it up, and experimenting to get the best results.

But it pays to point out the importance of the moment when the ballcarrier inside you is preparing to pass. At that moment your opponent may focus on him rather than you. This gives you the chance to:

(a) take the ball short – cut back inside him and carry the ball into space;
(b) take the ball long – swing outside him and take the longer pass in space.

Stress the idiocy of running flat, except as part of a carefully rehearsed plan, and the futility of trying to play rugby running back.

You cannot hope to apply starts mechanically. Even the simplest is dependent on the player exercising judgement in terms of positioning and timing. But once you've mastered the simple principles behind the effective use of space and time, and got over initial hesitancy in intervening, you'll find it easy enough. You'll find all you need to know below in Part Four. Aim to clarify for the players the timings that will make the start effective; not giving it away by starting too early, or creating unnecessary pressure by starting too late.

2. ASSIGN STARTS TO SITUATIONS

The staple activity is the expression of our *strategy*: what suits us best; what we practise most; what we feel greatest confidence in; what we happily revert to when there's no immediate cue for another form of attack.

Situations are the basis of our *tactics* – the ways in which we seek to exploit particular opportunities. Situations are based on *tactical points* (scrums, line-outs, rucks and mauls where we take the ball in and are reasonably sure of getting it back, penalties, fair catches, kick-offs). We know that these TPs are going to occur in particular areas of the pitch, probably in every match and certainly in any short sequence of matches. Each one offers us the chance to plan and practise the most effective form of attack for our particular team at that point.

It is inevitable that at each point a decision will be made. The only question is whether we clarify our options in the comparative peace and leisure of the practice, define what we're going to do, and practise it so that every player knows how he's going to contribute, or whether we defer our decisions to the heat and haste of the match. Do we make absolutely clear to ourselves and the players what our particular team is best equipped to do in that situation, or do we neglect the opportunity and hope that our players can work out answers on the spur of the moment?

The beauty of *this* approach is its preparedness: the TDM can assess it very quickly. As a tactical point approaches – as he predicts that our centre will be tackled, but will keep possession, any moment now, 15m from their line with about 20m blind-side on his right – he's able to draw on an accustomed *model*, knowing that their defensive line-up is completely predictable.

His *feedback* from the matches gives him a line on forward strength; let's say it confirms the likelihood of our getting the ball back. It may also have indicated particular strengths or weaknesses in the opposing defence.

He already has *expectations* of where there are liable to be system weaknesses in their defence: their left wing is a lonely figure in a lot of space, and the rest of their back three may be coming across to cover. No – so that's a good place to strike, and the *action* we're best equipped to take is just that. So he makes his call, a call that was expected by those most concerned because they too can read the signs, and the team moves into a very purposeful attack. The coach feels pretty good, too; he knows damn well that if we win the ruck there we're 90% certain to score. I won't bore you with reminiscences of moments like that, but they abound, and they're very comforting.

There are always variables – relative pack strength, the weather, a player being absent or off form – but these may actually simplify the tactical decision by ruling out certain gambits.

And it's utterly practical: it's been worked out in practices, tested in practices and previous matches, refined in practices; it's familiar. If the TDM has doubts, he falls back on what the team have been doing best. If he gets bad ball, he's been trained to prepare for it: as soon as he calls, he's deciding what he as an individual will do if bad ball rules out the first choice. He may have to kick, but he'll kick with a purpose; he may go himself, intent on getting in front of the pack if he can, and close to support if he can't. He's got a system working for him that reminds him what to do. It's a good system for making the most of possession.

It isn't exactly new. Most teams already do something like this. Once they get into the 22, they're thinking of back-row moves, or hoping to drop a goal. All we're doing is clarifying the process, and relating the team repertoire more precisely to recurrent and representative situations. As coach, you start with *critical* situations: pick out one situation from which you should be able to score; think about it in terms of your team; enlist their ideas, out on the pitch, exactly at that point; come to a decision in terms of your particular strengths . . . and you're on your way.

It's very likely that at first you'll be working wholly inside your existing repertoire. It's true that most teams would benefit from extending the range of their repertoire, especially in terms of variants to get the ball back into their strategic strike channel – but there's evidently a point at which variety becomes an embarrassment. What you *are* doing is deploying your repertoire most effectively.

Much of your existing repertoire will operate in a range of situations, but you may decide to limit the range of strike for maximum effect. A peel round the front of the line-out, for example, can be effective in attack anywhere in their half of the field; but if you save it till you're 5 or 10m out, you may score.

We can work out an example in terms of a standard start – say a back-row move to the left. These tend to be a little more cross-field than attacks to the right, so you stipulate a minimum of 15–20m of space to the left.

You work out in practice an effective range for this, which depends, of course, on the speed of your back row relative to the defenders they'll be playing against. You then decide, let's say on a strike from inside their 22. You are now defining a situation:

- a scrum, our put-in;
- just inside their 22;
- 15–20–25 yards of space to the left.

You always need alternative actions to cover the possibility that your pack will be under pressure, but that's less important here: a degree of wheel may be to your advantage. So you can add:

- even when under pressure up front.

In preparation, you work out how to clear the channel of attack. In this case, your fullback drifts discreetly, but not too discreetly – wide on the right, just outside our centres, and our left wing moves out to touch. As soon as the call is made, they get out there. The TDM doesn't need to worry about setting things up: all the players know what's going to happen; they've been expecting it since the scrum was awarded, as one choice from perhaps three. What tilted the TDM in favour of this start is feedback from earlier in the game, and earlier in the season: our back row has an edge; the opposing centres are very effective in defence, or their drift defence has soaked up our overlap attempts; their right wing is limping. Whatever is relevant.

You can see the system at work here: model of the situation; feedback on the players; expectations of what will work; actions grooved in practice. You can see that the situation is likely to occur. You can see the value of central control in making the final choice, of all the team being involved. It carries no guarantee of success, but it certainly reduces the odds against us.

It has a further benefit: we're less likely to squander the ball. For example, an opponent has got in front of their drop-out 22; you've been awarded a scrum in the centre of their 22m line. It's a situation from which you ought to score; it's a situation so certain to arise that you must prepare for it. Your fly-half should drop a goal . . . but *your* fly-half can't be depended upon to drop a goal, and anyway, the wind's strong and gusting. You have a couple of alternatives planned, practised, ready to use and simply waiting for the call. You have the whole team focusing its energy on a known method of achieving its objective.

You can also see that this process will focus your attention on gaps in your repertoire. It would, for example, be very useful if your fly-half *could* be depended upon to drop goals – and that surely falls within your remit as coach.

If the happy day comes when you have a full game-plan, you will have answers like that above worked out to cover attack and defence in a wide variety of situations (each kind of tactical point at representative loci on the pitch). Evidently, however, you want to start with the most critical, say 5m out from the line, and the most probable, for example KO and receiving KO.

Does it work? One of our graduates, then coaching a very successful local senior club 1st XV (and now called to higher things), talked it over two seasons ago, adopted the back-row attack model above, and had 100% success with it over the rest of the season. Like everything else in the book, it's based on successful practice. It requires a more carefully focused effort, but it brings a high return. An example of how you might inspect such a situation, and the kind of thinking that guides *your* thinking, is given in Part Four.

This setting up is simply the first stage, however, and to leave it there as a theoretical possibility that you expect the TDM and team to employ when it might fit is ridiculous. Once you've set it up, you have to take it out and practise it hard, really working on the detail, and then incorporate it into unopposed programmes of one kind or other, so that it comes to be associated with reaching a certain area on the pitch. Then you can play it in a conditioned form to let the TDM begin to respond to actual cues.

A great benefit of this is a very clear sense of purpose in the practice. Each one of these critical or representative situations you cover is one more step towards highly integrated team play in which your team will have a very clear advantage in terms of speed, efficiency and appropriateness of action.

3. UNIT RHYTHMS OR SEQUENCES

Once we've established the best starting positions, relevant timings and proper angles of run, we need to habituate the players to the call and improve their discipline and speed in implementing it. We can do this with what I originally called a *unit rhythm*.

This consists of a set series of tactical points which can be repeated in cyclic fashion. The key idea is that the rhythm should reflect your basic team patterns and tactics. For example, the back division of a team that seeks to strike at first centre might work on a rhythm: *scrum on right . . . switch between stand-off and centre . . . maul on gain-line (part one) . . . maul on gain-line . . . attack left with fullback in . . . out to wing (part two).* That brings us to the mid-point of the rhythm, which is immediately repeated in the opposite direction. You will see this clearly in the diagram (Fig. 11). We are seeking to establish *accelerated response*:

- speed of call, and habit of call;
- discipline in positioning;
- discipline in timing;
- sense of space and expectation of sequence.

It would be excellent practice to work out precisely the coaching points you'd make for this model, and the weaknesses you'd expect; and it would be very valuable to sit down now and design a rhythm for your own team, reflecting its basic strategy and tactics.

You start by running through slowly, arranging, explaining, getting the timing right. The first aim is not speed but accuracy: we need to establish our criteria of successful performance. Emphasise particularly the need for the scrum-half to control the tempo at the mauls: to let them get into position, and to wait for the stand-off's signal.

You develop it by:

- increasing the speed – we want the scrum-half finally to check and be able to pass at once;

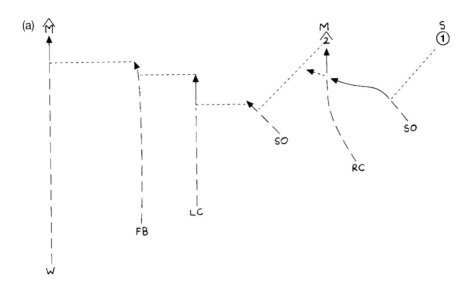

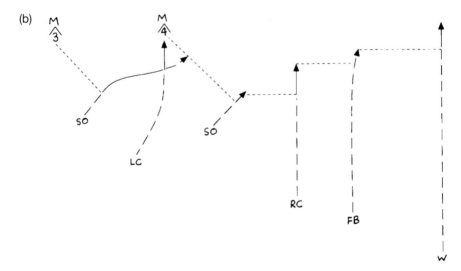

***Fig. 11* A typical 'sequence' or 'rhythm'**
(a) Practise the sequence going left.
(b) Immediately repeat the sequence going right. 'Immediately' means 'as soon as you are in shape to try it with a fair chance of success'. The SH controls the tempo, and you all aim to reduce the time he has to wait. Start slow, and polish for speed.

- moving on to two (or three) complete cycles as a continuous activity – a great test of conditioning as well as discipline;
- incorporating more difficult material – for example, starts requiring two-stage timing from the scrum-half;
- building in cues for decisions – for example, having a wing in opposition on part two who goes in to take fullback, or stays out with wing.

I've found that four basic kinds of rhythm work well:

(i) Coach-dictated – reflecting his sense of what is needed this week with these particular opponents coming up, or to reinforce patterns.

(ii) TDM-dictated – to make him think about space and timing, and to force appropriate calls.

(iii) Either (i) or (ii) with the back-row working on support roles to set up mauls/rucks. This is best done once the coach is happy with the performance of the backs, and can concentrate on back-row movement.

(iv) Using it as a basis for full team unopposed.

Increasingly, I've come to see this practice as a very valuable way of introducing the TDM to the cues associated with a particular choice of action. And I've come to think of them as 'sequences' – the kind of continuation you might expect to be successful from a given opening. To take a very clear example: *scrum on right . . . miss to outside centre . . . maul on gain line (part one) . . . maul on gain line . . .* either *scrum-half breaks blind . . . maul on left* or *scrum-half chips for left wing (part two) and repeat.* (To make sure of continuity you may find it useful to park a spare ball where you expect to start repeating the rhythm, so that a loose chip doesn't check the whole thing.)

Now you introduce a cue for the scrum-half that will trigger the most effective action. If the opposing winger is back, he can attack by handling; if he's up, the scrum-half can chip behind him.

This is a great exercise. Make it clear what the TDM should look for, and offer the appropriate cue. Or work through it with him: at the first check ask him what he'd call and work out with all the players what the key cues are. Then provide them using the coach or reserves to indicate opposition choices. You will find the raw material of many appropriate sequences in Part Five – basically a way of striking in your strategic channel followed by a way of striking in the remaining space.

4. THE MOVING FINGER

If you want a greater variety than that afforded by sequences, try the moving finger, which moves on fairly rapidly.

It's a device I've used for the backs as a unit, rather than for the team, and it's ridiculously simple. The coach moves around the ground with the ball. As he moves, the backs are falling into position behind him. He puts the ball down, puts a finger on it, and yells 'scrum' or 'ruck' or whatever. The TDM calls, the scrum-half controls the tempo and calls for the ball as soon as the backs are in position. The backs play through the call. Everyone trots back to the starting point and the coach moves on his way, complete with ball.

Of course, it's a coaching situation. It's a device for checking appropriateness of call, speed of call, speed into position, and efficiency of play. But it can be a pleasant, light-hearted exercise as well.

5. UNOPPOSED AND SEMI-OPPOSED RUGBY

This most basic and flexible of team coaching devices has much to offer. You'll find detail on the techniques you can use in *Total Rugby*. It's an excellent way of creating confidence in our ability to move through a sequence of play fast and accurately, and it gives the coach a great chance to review and revise team development. Look at the short account in Part One of how to do this most effectively.

Tactically, we are concerned with four conditioned variations, three of which were devised purely to give intensive calling practice, or intensive predictive practice. Their great beauty is that they do this while keeping the whole team active and improving.

i. Programmed unopposed

The whole sequence of attacks is dictated beforehand by the coach, but is called by the TDM. The sequence embodies basic responses to various *situations*, and creates a sense of team rhythms. It helps if the coach keeps close to the TDM and talks him through it. The talk is mainly questions: 'What cues you to do this? Look for the wing: are you happy with his position? What's your provisional alternative?' The coach has to display the habit of mind he wants the TDM to adopt. But like the TDM, the coach can start with the easy things, and develop.

ii. Thematic unopposed

In this we take as our theme a single tactical point, and we play appropriate variations from it all the way down the pitch. It becomes an intensive situation practice starting from a line-out, or a penalty, or a scrum (rucks and mauls appear incidentally and are usually called, and you can call them as often and wherever you want).

The aim is to improve the accuracy of call by accustoming the TDM to the changes called for by the different locations, and to accelerate the team response.

Line-out

Put a ball at each line down the pitch, about 10m from touch (all you need is a couple of balls and a willing reserve to make sure the next position has a ball).

Start on the deadball line with a call for the first line-out *so that all the forwards know what's on*. It has to be *appropriate* – just what you'd do in the match – and it has to be *quickly implemented* with every forward scampering into the right position.

It's immediately followed by an appropriate call from your TDMs. You play through second-phase (with you calling the ruck or maul), and then it's straight to the next line, the next call, the next line-out. You get the early call, the fast response, the appropriate team call, speed into position, efficient implementation, and you're on to the next line, the next ball, the next line-out.

Penalty

Take a couple of minutes to plot on a pitch-outline the probable distribution of the different kicks at your disposal. *Kicks at goal* will fall into a shape dictated by the kicker's accurate range. Yes, he may occasionally put one over outside that area, but every time you ask him to kick and he fails you're lowering his confidence, and possibly (though not necessarily) wasting possession. *Up and unders* can be marvellously effective if they're accurate in height, direction, and length. Where do you do them from, and where do you want the ball to land? *Kicks to touch:* very useful with the wind behind, and the near certainty of recovering possession at the following line-out. But can you? If not, a long kick *down touch* may be a far better bet. Where from? *Tap penalties:* often fail, because they're inadequately prepared, and applied without judgement. Where do you want to play them? What will you do close to the right touch? Close to the left touch? In midfield? Close to their line? Plot your answers on the pitch diagram. What you've got now is a model to present for discussion to individual players, and then the team. Once it's agreed, get on that pitch and take penalties as your theme. Start with your players on your goal-line, and award a penalty right in the middle of the 22. Get the fast call, and the fast team response: you want everyone in the right position (as a minimum, behind the ball) as the sound of the whistle dies away. Play the call, and carry on as if it were your ball. For example, it's gone into touch, take the throw, play the call, call for a ruck, award a penalty . . . and so on right down the pitch, so that the TDM and the team learn to respond *appropriately*, *fast and accurately*. You'll end up 5m from the opposition line with a penalty from which you must score.

Scrums

An easy way of doing this is to go 'down the sides and up the middle', with a ball ready on the next line each time. 'Down the sides', the ball will be on the intersection of the next line and the 15m line; 'up the middle', on the centre of each line. You can vary these, of course, especially if you want a little more space on the blind-side. You play it exactly as you would the line-out.

Throughout these practices you're concentrating on the speed of call. It's a little artificial, as any unopposed practice must be, but it's extremely effective. Remember that the practice will always be more effective if you've prepared for it. If you've doubts about the team's ability to carry out a tap penalty effectively, work on it before you start the intensive practice. Try not to stop in the middle of a run: keep your comments, or desire to go through it again, till you get to the end.

iii. Indicated unopposed

This is a form of unopposed which concentrates the TDM's attention on how to attack at a particular point. He is free to call, but he must direct each attack at the coach. The coach running ahead of play takes up a position that indicates a weakness, a suitable strike point.

At the start, get the scrum-half to pay particular attention to tempo control, and ask the TDM to call only from each first-phase start. You build in positions suitable for attack by the forwards as well, and this will help both halves to clarify their responsibilities.

The coach moves to his fresh position while the maul/ruck is in progress, and the scrum-half calls for the ball when everyone is ready. You want, as always, to move towards a higher tempo, and to calls in second- as well as first-phase. And as always, you check occasionally to establish that the TDM has a provisional alternative worked out.

iv. Predictive unopposed

Up to now, the TDM has been responsible for every tactical call in all the varieties of unopposed. This time he takes over responsibility for every call – including calling for each tactical point. This forces him to stay constantly attentive to events, figuring ahead, reckoning the probabilities, preparing to exploit the situation.

The main job for the coach at the start of this is to encourage the TDM to be realistic; to make a realistic estimate of what would happen. There's a temptation for him to choose what he'd like to happen, rather than what's on the cards, and to set up situations he can handle easily rather than those most likely to occur. Encourage him to show just how well he understands the game, how capably he can predict what's likely to happen in the course of this phase of attack. Most players merely need to be given a better target, a better challenge.

These four varieties of unopposed (or semi-unopposed, for you can easily introduce a token opposition) aim to exercise quite basic functions:

- trust in our staple activity, and a clearer sense of how to proceed in particular situations;
- eliciting a very fast response to a given stimulus so that a very fast call and a fast implementation are possible;
- attention to weaknesses in the opposition, and selecting a way to exploit it; and
- always thinking ahead and forecasting what's likely to happen – what the next tactical point will be, and where.

I've never set out to impose any of these patterns, or to suggest that we simply transfer them to match play. They are method practices rather than simply content practices, designed to encourage attitudes rather than simple obedience. It's fair to say, however, that it pays to limit the choices at any point, as we've done in one or two of these practices. The TDM can suffer, like Buridan's ass or myself in Marks & Spencer, from too wide a range of choice as from one too restricted. Too few options can lead to a loss of initiative; too many to a mental paralysis. We need to establish:

- a *representative repertoire* – starts that between them exploit the attacking power of all sections of the team;
- a *'certain' repertoire* – starts so effective for our team that they'll figure in the majority of our matches;
- a *critical repertoire* – starts designed to exploit situations from which we should be able to score; and
- a *staple activity* – into which various of the starts above will fit to disguise our purpose.

Your team probably has a representative repertoire – the most basic. You can see that the others are more specific and more important. Establishing them requires the thought of the whole team; they should then be reduced to fit as precisely as possible to the recurring situations. Your TDM should have clear expectations of what's on – possibly two or three starts – as the impending situation gets clearer. More than that, and inefficiency sets in.

6. CONDITIONED UNIT UNOPPOSED

We've used various devices to supply a clue as to opposition defensive set-ups: basically a single coach/player to represent a weakness, or a single opposition player, or a limited opposition to pose less predictable problems. But we will benefit from supplying the TDM with specific cues to look for in the opposing defence.

I. The isolated defender

The isolated defender is always weak. The reason for defensive systems is that each player supports and reinforces the others. However, the pattern of the game does tend to impose weakness on some players.

The winger

He has always two roles to play, one in depth defence and one as a tackler, and he buys efficiency in one at the cost of inefficiency in the other. At every tactical point with a blind-side the scrum-half should check up on the positioning of the opposing winger: usually he can be attacked by chipping in behind him if he's up, or by a short attack if he's back. This must enter into your situation preparations.

The centre

When centres split, with the wing lying back to cover touch, one centre is often left isolated and open to attack. This situation is an ideal cue for attack from your own goal-line as long as you are moderately skilful.

Once again, this is a cue to the coach to set up an intensive situation practice, establishing the positions and lines of run that will make for successful attack. This means repetition till the TDM automatically checks what the opposition are doing. I've seen some lovely tries from this start.

The fullback

In a poorly organised side, or with a strong wind in his face, the fullback can become isolated. If he drops back to cover the long kick he may:

- leave space in front of him that can be exploited by chips over with our front three up flat and running. This area is often patrolled by the No. 8, and it helps if you have checked him earlier on (for example by chipping back over his head or attacking close). Design a sequence to set this up as a team possibility;

- get isolated from the wingers, so that a fumble will be doubly difficult: test him with high kicks (and have the front three following up from a flat position in line); or

- call one of his wingers back to help. He buys strength at the cost of weakness against a fast handling attack aimed at that wing.

Of course, if he stays up, he's asking for trouble from the least tactically gifted of half-backs.

ii. System weaknesses

Any system buys strength in one area at the cost of weakness elsewhere, and if you give your TDMs cues to look for they can spot the weakness and exploit it.

Pressure defence

This seeks to push forward and pressure the attack into mistakes. You can outflank them: do miss-passes to get the ball wide; run up the blind-side. You can use the space behind them: chip over their heads wide to outside centre and winger. You can attack inside them: scrum-half and back-row.

A special case of pressure defence is the very tight front three often used by the All Blacks (perhaps because they get used to close attacks), which leaves a lot of space wide.

Drift defence

This is my phrase for the defence used against wide attack, and often at line-outs, to cover an extra man coming in: each player stands a little wider than normal, and takes the player one out. Stand-off looks after first centre, and so on. This buys strength wide at the expense of weakness at stand-off: we must be able to focus attack there, with fast support to take the ball away from the back row.

You may find it convenient to delegate the spotting of defence systems to whoever is on the blind-side wing: after two or three attacks, it should be moderately clear what they're doing and, therefore, where to attack.

iii. Personal weaknesses

No system is stronger than the weakest link. If the opposition have a player who won't tackle or is a weak tackler, one who is injured or is a replacement, or one who is out of position, you must attack him. For the coach, it's a matter of establishing lines of communication: the TDM must be kept aware of the possibilities.

Rugby teams are not famed for good communication. Too often, after complete silence on the pitch, a player will come off claiming that if he'd been given the ball, he could have run round/over/through his opponent because the latter was scared to tackle/injured/out of position. Such messages must reach the TDM on the field.

It may well help if the information is processed before delivery, particularly if it's a request rather than raw information. 'Chip it in behind him' is that much simpler than 'he's slow on the turn'.

All of the above categories of weakness can be acted out by presenting a conditioned defence for the TDM and players to inspect. Play each one as a single situation and repeat it until you have eliminated mistakes. Initially you may exaggerate the weakness to make it stand out, but you've got to reduce it to a realistic level. Again, you needn't concentrate all your attention on the TDM: all the players should become aware of the significant cues for action, though only one will make the call.

7. OPPOSED SITUATIONS

For a long time I questioned the practicability of opposed practice, 1st XV v 2nd XV, because it always threatened to become personal. However, the next two steps both involve team against team.

By limiting the time-scale severely, you can achieve intensity without the frustrations of fatigue or repeated setbacks; by giving both teams the chance to attack and defend you can keep team objectives to the forefront, and relegate personal objectives to the background.

The first step is an opposed version of the work done on situations. There are in-built difficulties: your opponents, for example, ought to know pretty well what you intend to do. (If they don't, your reserve strength is weaker than it need be. You must expect to lose players through injury, and you need as far as possible to slot reserves into the vacancies. To do that, they need to know exactly how you play.) You should see this as merely an added challenge, but if it threatens to cause trouble, it's worthwhile switching defending players out of position to create something like match conditions.

The exercise is simple: you select the situation you want to practise, and you give each team three, four, or five opportunities to attack or defend. The better they become, the fewer repetitions they need. You play through second-phase, or to a score.

It puts great emphasis on raising the team effort for a short period, and stresses the need for the individual to exert 100% effort in the immediate situation. This corresponds to those vital three-minute spells of maximum effort after any score, at the beginning and end of each half, and when within a few metres of a goal-line. If you can raise your game at those moments you'll put up your success rate at once.

A typical situation to take is a 'critical' – a scrum, say 5 or 10m from the line, 15–20m in from touch – which affords immediate clear objectives for both teams. The attackers must get across; the defenders must keep them out this time . . . and this time . . . and this time. It reveals the basic truth: we can raise our chances considerably by planning how best to use our resources, but it's the commitment, the sheer determination of the individual player within our plans that makes them work.

It's an easy step to move on to a sequence which you already know well in unopposed. Your initial strike (which leads in the sequence to a second tactical point) is aimed at complete penetration and a score, but you know if checked exactly how we intend to strike in second phase.

Within both these practices, you should hammer home absolutely basic ideas. The most important in the critical situations concerns the striker: you go 100% out for a score, and as soon as you're checked your only aim is to get that ball back. These are basic priorities for the team: score, and never give away the ball.

8. THREE-MINUTE RUGBY

Opposed situations give intensive practice of basic attack plans, and defence plans. They make us face the difficulties, and give us the chance and motivation to put things right. After each run, one side or the other is going to take a time-out to thrash out difficulties. It's a coaching situation that reveals radical truths about what we're capable of doing.

Three-minute rugby aims at the same intensity of effort but on a wider front: instead of concentrating on a single situation it offers a very limited time in which to achieve objectives. Think of these three minutes as the last three in a match, with the result depending on whether the team in possession can score, or whether the defending team can hold out.

You start in different situations, a variety of distances from the line. You will find out a lot about the optimum range of attack for your team. They may well find it easier to make decisive breaks further out from the line than the critical situations we've looked at. As they move away from their line the defenders have more and more space to cover, and offer different opportunities to the attack. You will also establish maximum effective distances for some forms of attack. To take an obvious example: you've organised an effective peel round the front of your line-out; what's the range over which our particular player has the odds in his favour of reaching the line before the cover catches him or forces him out?

The exercise also reinforces the value of staying cool under pressure of time. Three minutes is a long time if you are always ahead of the play, making intelligent calls; it's a very short time if you're inefficient in calling or in execution.

And it also reinforces the need to be able to play with great intensity for those short but critical spells we've already detailed.

As with opposed situations, you have to see them as coaching situations: an opportunity to see how things work under high pressure, and to explain and amend what goes wrong.

These eight steps form a programme which will certainly improve the coherence of your play, and reduce drastically waste of possession, provided you are committed to quality control and supply energy in the early stages. Players are converted by success: show them success and they'll offer you commitment.

They also offer a development programme for your back play. It's a weird irony that many players who show the greatest talent for the game are among the forgotten 47%, the neglected 47%, those to whom the coach doesn't offer effective guidance because he doesn't understand how to help them. If he gets to understand Part Four of this book, absorbs the relevant chapters in *Total Rugby*, and applies these exercises, the coach can't help but right the balance in their favour.

But the great thing is that the entire programme isn't additional to what's done now: it's simply a more efficient replacement for it. The players find that there's a great deal more being done in the same amount of time, and that they're learning more rapidly. The person who has to work a bit harder is the coach, but the reward is enhanced status: he obviously does have a programme; he knows where the team are going; he's got ideas and means of carrying them out.

6 **Preparing the TDM**

Most players rely on particular abilities, are happiest in particular situations, and contribute to the team through these abilities. Your TDMs, however, need a wider range of aptitudes, and need to deploy them in accord with the most essential criterion of all – judgement of team needs. It's evident that a technical weakness at the centre of team play can effectively reduce the options open to the team much more radically than the same weakness in a peripheral player. It's evident, too, that doing the wrong thing, no matter how skilfully, has an equally exaggerated effect when the decision concerns the whole of an attack, and not merely a single player's contribution.

These points, like the prospect of defeat, should concentrate the coach's mind wonderfully. It's evident in view of the first point that time spent improving the technical abilities of the halves is never wasted, and that the coach should think in terms of establishing for them a personal programme of self-coaching. If you can get them to spend ten minutes each session on clearly organised work, they'll begin to improve. Working together they can have intensive practice of most aspects of their game.

Take kicking, for example. Get the scrum-half to put three or four balls on a line parallel to the goal-line, in goal, behind the posts. That line can represent the back of a scrum or ruck. He starts from the goal-line, as if he's put the ball into the scrum there, nips back and kicks over the crossbar to the stand-off. The stand-off may be in a particular position to help him practise a particular kick (for example, back into the box), or be moving around to give a different target. The scrum-half works hard on getting quick height to clear the crossbar – the opposing flankers – and accuracy. He then aims for speed, kicking, going back to the goal-line, nipping back to kick again, and so on down the line of balls, Meanwhile, the stand-off (and possibly the fullback) is fielding the kicks, and in turn kicking at a clear target: to drop the ball where it came from. (You'll see that other players might also benefit from such a practice, and in particular the back three. They have to be adept at covering against kicks and clearing under pressure. So you adapt the practice to take in all four. You have two providing the targets and kicking back accurately to player three, while player four does the specific practice. Then they all rotate. You have one player in charge, encouraging high quality standards and keeping everyone active. So you set up a cyclic exercise which guarantees intensive practice, while you are busy elsewhere. Of course, you go through it first in detail, and you keep an eye on it from wherever you happen to be.)

Another example is an exercise to improve speed of positioning and pass. They start off with the ball on the 22, and the stand-off takes up a position he has decided on for a particular purpose. The scrum-half feeds him. The stand-off runs on to the ball, and does a short, controlled grubber. The scrum-half chases it, checks it and prepares to feed. Meanwhile the stand-off is moving into his next position, intent on getting it right but seeking to minimise delay by the scrum-half.

Ten minutes spent following a programme of this kind, either suggested by experiences in the last match or preparing for particular problems in the next, can do a power of good. Those ten minutes could be spent footling around to no purpose. Of course, the coach may need that kind of ten-minute spell to put something right between the halves. If they have a habit of turning out together, it's very easy to do that important work before the rest of the players need attention.

If only one can turn out, it's an excellent chance to spend ten minutes tying him up with the partner he'd get if the other half were unavailable for a match. And if no one else is there, you could have him increasing the power of his kicking by blasting the ball into the roof of the adjacent soccer net.

The point made at the start, however, remains to be answered: what about the half who behaves like an ordinary player – who has a preferred skill, and uses it to a degree that distorts team tactics? Or who has gambits that he especially favours? As a coach you'll quickly become aware of this: you simply won't see the team functioning as you've prepared it to function. What you need to do is:

- convince the player that he has to satisfy a demanding audience – the coach, and the rest of the team;

- convince him that the single most important criterion of his success is right judgement in deploying the resources of the team – it's that, and not, for example, his kicking or his elusive running, which is his cardinal virtue;

- show him proof of how he has used the ball – do a little analysis as detailed in *Total Rugby*, pp. 81–2 or above p. 30;

- talk through with the team questions implied by the reliance on a restricted set of gambits – perhaps the team has real doubts about some that he isn't using, or particular trust in those he is. (Personally, though, I'd tactfully insist that the gambits we'd worked on should be given a fair chance!)

To this, in the most difficult case, you may have to add a little more. The most difficult cases I've come across concern players who feel a need to be seen, who depend to some extent on games performance for self-approval. They aren't, of course, typical, but they can be very troublesome: they tend to absorb more time than the coach can spare. You must aim to reassure such a player as a person; express liking and respect for him as a person; enlist the help of those you can trust to continue the campaign in your absence; and go on repeating that the right audience to play for consists of those whose opinion really counts, and that the great virtue is judgement.

The other course is simply to drop him. This is complicated by the fact that his rugby means so much to him. I don't think you should ever 'simply' drop a player: every player deserves an account of the precise reasons behind his being dropped, and an account of what he has to improve to get back in the team. Every player who has been dropped will benefit from being made to feel just as important as a person as he was while in the team. Just telling him the kind of exercises to do, the kind of personal practices to set up, is a step in the right direction. These points are all the more important with the player in the difficult case above.

THE COACH AND SELECTION

This is a suitable point at which to make more detailed comment on how to select, and when to drop.

As a coach, you come to recognise that the only way to achieve consistent success is to work towards long-term objectives. Just as it's unlikely that you can create an instantly successful pattern in team play, so it's unlikely that you can create an instant team by selection alone. The two things go together in a continuing programme of team development. The good coach is very close to the players, and in a position to know about their strengths and weaknesses at first hand and through the opinions of the other players. You're constantly seeking to use the strengths and to set right the weaknesses.

This process will start for the talented individual player before he reaches the 1st XV: you know you're going to use him, and you want to be sure that when the time comes he'll be up to it. And it should continue with the player in the XV: to discard a player for a technical weakness is a sad comment on your coaching before he reached the team and during his stay in it. Yet it happens even at the highest level of play, if not of coaching: a player is picked for his country because he's brilliant in attack, and dropped because he can't defend. Next season starts: he's still brilliant in attack; he still can't defend. Do his club and national coach think the weakness will just go away? That he'll grow out of it? Do the selectors feel so surrounded by talent that they needn't waste their time with him? Do the national organisers of coaching ever note that there's a problem to be set right, and that it would be a marvellous theme for summer courses? For the genuine coach, dropping a player is a last resort.

This is largely because he is working long term and continuously. Long before season's end, he is projecting next year's team, identifying potential new players, identifying possible gaps, establishing as realistically as he can what the team will be, and what the reserve team will be. This is done well because there's no immediate pressure and because the coach has time to start preparing the new characters. He'll invite them to join the practice, pay special attention to them, give a little time to suggesting practices, get to know them. It's far better to be sure that they're going to fit the position, the demands of the level of rugby, and the need to function happily as part of the team, than to pick them and drop them. Creating a team is an organic process rather than a mechanical one.

Once this process is under way, it's common sense to remain loyal to the players that you've chosen with care, and prepared for their role. Even if they don't play well, they're still the most likely – if you yourself are capable – to do well. If the final XV showed more than a couple of unenforced changes from the team that originally I had projected, I'd be a little disappointed.

This manner of working also allows you to offer long-term advice to players. Often this concerns change of position, and preparation for a change of position. You can see that certain qualities and abilities suggest he'll be able to function at a certain level, but that at that level he'll fit in best in a different position – for example, as a scrum-half rather than a flanker, as a hooker rather than a prop, as a prop rather than a lock, and so on. This is miles away from the precipitate decision to throw him into that position, or to get him to change because it looks as if the team can use him there next week. I've seen excellent players treated like this by their clubs and denied a proper run at international level as a result. Of course, there will be times when you ask a player to change position because the team needs it: even the best preparation doesn't guarantee success. But if so, the player ought to feel that he can trust you – that you recognise what you're asking, and that he won't suffer from it.

At the top level, though, where you have adequate time to practise, it pays to accustom all your players to a variety of positions. Just as the forwards have been released from constricting stereotypes, so the backs should recognise that the more adaptive they are – the more they become a 'complete back' – the greater the contribution they can make to the team and their own career. Interchangability is the coming thing in back play.

One consideration in inviting a player to join the practice must be the way in which he and the coach get along. People shy away from this, thinking in terms of crude favouritism or unfairness, but it's a clear factor in the smooth, efficient running of the team. It's especially important, of course, with captains. It's becoming increasingly obvious that the coach supplies much of the continuity to team development, and that if he's good he's much harder to replace than a captain. The appointment of the captain, therefore, must take into consideration the need to work well with the coach. The simplest clear statement of the captain's position is that he represents the coach on the field of play. Evidently, he can't do this if he's out of tune with the coach's purposes. I've only once had this happen, and that pained me for a whole season.

All being well, however, this possibility can be avoided by long-term preparation. No coach can run a practice single-handed. There will always be times when he has to devote his entire attention to a single problem, when he has to spend a disproportionate time with one unit, when he may not even be able to turn up for the practice. To cover these times, he needs to accustom players to coaching responsibilities. It pays to have players in charge of units and sub-units. You give them a list of what you want that group to do – not general aims but specific practices – and they're responsible for getting it done. If you look up and they're not hard at work, well . . . This isn't merely an organisational expedient, it's a grand way of establishing whether they show leadership, of accustoming them to take charge, and of letting the other players see their potential.

The first two help prepare the player as captain, and the third helps get him elected as captain. Personally, I've always started the players thinking about the following year's captain as soon as I start thinking about the following year's team. There's no reason why their decision should be less leisurely and thought-out than my own. What I want to happen is an unopposed election of the person I see as best for the position. It's possibly worth adding, however, that no one is more committed to the club's success than I am, and the players can see this!

Something of the same applies to the coaching and preparation of the TDM. There's no quick way of establishing him as TDM: he too has to show leadership, has to become accustomed to exercising a tactical function, has to be accepted by the other players. The earlier you start creating the opportunity for these elements to operate, the better. Not every half who reaches you will recognise his tactical function and accept tactical responsibilities. I've known one player – a grand lad, with fine personal skills – who found it impossible to accept the role of director of operations. The result was that many of our gambits remained in abeyance: we played as if we had a very restricted repertoire. To some extent, I had to accept responsibility for this: I simply hadn't managed to prepare him enough. But on the whole it was right to leave him out. It would have required too great an investment of time to get him operating effectively.

FUNCTIONS OF THE CAPTAIN

The bulk of tactical decisions are made by players in set positions. The captain may not be one of them. So what *is* his job?

1. *The hero figure* – of different styles according to the club – who still feels the score can be improved in the fourth minute of injury time; who feels if he gives enough he can take the opposition on single-handed; who gives more for the team than he could possibly give for himself.

2. *The immediate motivator* – of different styles according to the club – who strengthens the weak, inspires the faint-hearted, celebrates the strong and expects 100% from everybody.

3. *The technical director* – who is the coach's right-hand man in sharing responsibility for the smooth functioning and high work-rate of the practice; who is responsible for implementing team policy on the field; who is responsible for quality control in the team at large but especially in his unit.

4. *The master of ceremonies* before, during and after the match – who arranges

courtesies for referee and visitors; who maintains good relations with referee and visitors on the field; who sees to it that everyone is taken care of after the match.

Every club should look at the possibility of having a club captain as well as a team captain – to take as much administration as possible off the team captain's shoulders, and to act as ombudsman for club members.

'SPECIFIC TACTICAL TALENT'

Amongst the factors you try to assess in your search for the TDMs, and which you try to encourage (I haven't thought out ways of actually practising them yet), are three which I've lumped together under 'specific tactical talent'. The inverted commas are to suggest my doubts of its existence, even as some residual survival factor from a deer-hunting prehistory. It covers the following qualitative judgements and decisions (which are easier to delineate than to set up in practices).

The ability to spot the unexpected and respond to it effectively

It's obviously a little difficult to devise practices that cover the totally unexpected! In attack, this often calls for a personal response to a personal opportunity; a purely personal action, such as the sudden break by the stand-off who's been well-policed all the afternoon. But it's a far more remarkable feat to respond effectively to, say, a new defensive system: it may well be hard to spot, and to find answers to it in the heat of the moment is very demanding.

The ability to detect momentum and respond to it effectively

There are times when a team starts to roll – to develop a sustained attack, and impose sustained pressure.

On one occasion, we went into one match as complete underdogs. We then began to run them off their feet with rugby they'd never seen before, really enterprising rugby: we kept them off balance by throwing in unexpected attacks every time we got the ball, taking risks and playing with verve. Half-way through the second half we were well ahead. Then our TDM began to play safe, kicking for touch when we might have attacked. Immediately the opposition settled down to a game they knew, developing their momentum through larger, harder forwards. We went on simply trying to relieve the pressure rather than trying to raise the siege. They scored, and scored again, and eventually beat us. What the TDM has to do in attack is recognise what it is we're doing that's so successful, and carry on doing it. In defence, he has to recognise when relieving the pressure simply isn't enough, and an effort must be made to seize the initiative.

The ability to control tempo to the team's advantage

The TDM – often the scrum-half in this case – has to respond to the team's physical and emotional needs. He has got to settle the team so that it plays at its own tempo, not at a pace dictated by the opposition or imposed by its own nerves.

EXPLOITING YOUR OPPONENTS' EXPECTATIONS

This is one of those midway areas in which the coach can suggest and prepare, but the TDM has to judge, and judge things less concrete than the cues we've been working out for him.

Inevitably, like ourselves, our opponents are predicting what we'll do. They have expectations based on how we're known to play, and how they're seeing us play. One whole side of games playing sets out to exploit these expectations.

If we have a strategy, a staple activity, we can – as individual player, unit, or team – lead our opponents into assumptions about us. Our ability then to do the unexpected can be decisive. This has obvious implications for the coach: he must try to build in variations and alternatives, and specifically equip the team to shift the focus of its attack – for example from wide attacks to back row and blind-side – rapidly and efficiently. But the shift has to be in response to what's happening out there on the field; it's the responsibility of the TDM to throw the switch.

In the same way, it may pay a team to attack using the opponents' strategy. They won't expect it, because they won't be accustomed to it. A team renowned for its back play is rarely taken on at its own game, so it's often vulnerable to it. A team renowned for its forward play may be too formidable to take on head to head, but may be quite vulnerable to space attack by the forwards. And once again, someone on the pitch has to decide that the right moment has come.

Enterprising rugby creates its own expectations: 'They'll never repeat what they've just done.' But immediate repetition, repeating the same pressure, can be extremely effective, the more so as the opposition don't expect it. The most important assumptions, however, don't relate to specific teams, but to the game in general, and the probabilities within the game. What they reflect is a notion of risk-taking: 'They won't try anything here.' 'Here' is usually in or about your 22, where a mistake can indeed cost you dear. This inhibits many teams perfectly capable of accepting the risks involved.

The day before yesterday, I watched the stand-off of a team losing 11–6 kick a penalty to touch in the dying moments of a championship final, with a huge Olympic clock staring him in the face. He did the expected, and there was some reason for it: the opposition were very alert. Its defence had pressure, width, and depth. But the situation demanded risk-taking. Ten minutes earlier, it would have been sensible; in the last minute – the final whistle went as the ball sailed into touch – it was desperately negative. Some situations demand attack.

And there are many times during the game when attack from the 22 is certainly on. In fact, it calls for much the same kind of judgement as counter-attack; but with a little more time, if it's from a tactical point, to assess the odds. Here the coach can certainly help: first by preparing his team technically to the point where what would be an unacceptable risk for an ordinary team is perfectly acceptable for his (they won't make unforced errors); and secondly by clarifying the conditions where the opposition won't be able to force errors, for example:

- how well organised is their pressure defence? If we can get a 3 v 2 or better still a 2 v 1, there's something on;

- is there an isolated player? For example, from a scrum you'll often find that a wing drops back to cover touch, leaving a lonely centre who is vulnerable. This is precisely the kind of situation you should prepare for;

- can we clear a channel for attack, for example by our back row? That's the last thing they expect; and

- at our drop out, how well have they covered the pitch? This is a great opportunity *if you've prepared for it seriously*.

These guidelines aren't really enough. You need to show your stand-off what to look for, and what it should look like – and not just him, but all those involved. Success will depend on immediate cooperation.

Set up the reserves to show the typical positionings that create space which we can attack, from all the tactical points. Even if we can't make a decisive attack – by which I mean one we score from – we may at least be able to force them into finding touch rather than finding it ourselves close to our line. Get each situation clear, and practise, practise, practise.

You may benefit even more from their expectations if you reinforce them by apparently preparing to do what they expect – a penalty in your 22 or near their 22 that starts off by calling up your fullback will have some opponents turning their backs, and others relaxing – ideal for a handling attack. Of course, as you gain more of a reputation for the unexpected, your chances begin to diminish, but they never disappear.

All this willingness to take risks stems mainly from the coach. You have to create that sense of technical excellence that top players most enjoy – it's what motivates them most highly – and link it to a sense that if conditions are right they can score from behind their own line. And if things go wrong, you must support them, even if you have to go over once again the cues that really matter. But you never suggest that attack is always on: once you divorce skill from tactical judgement it'll never be wholly successful, and may be disastrous.

GETTING AND USING INFORMATION

There's a school of thought that suggests it's better to concentrate on one's own game than to worry about the opposition. I belong to it. However, that doesn't preclude responding very positively to any information you can glean about your opponents. Indeed, it would be ridiculous not to take account of any hard information you can get.

One source of such information is newspaper accounts of their games. This will put you in the picture about who scores tries, and how accurate their kickers are. It may well indicate who has played at a higher level, and it is possible that it will describe how they scored. You may also have access to video footage.

The other source is actually to go and watch them, or send people to watch them. If you can give precise points to monitor – your expectations of strength and weakness – you can get hard information back.

Usually, I've found this much more helpful in terms of our defence than our attack. If you know that their fullback, for example, comes in outside their winger, you can arrange a reception party to discourage him – for example, outside centre and fullback. But almost any piece of information can help, such as that their fullback is right-footed, and so we'll kick to his left.

This information should be processed. There's little point in presenting the players with raw material for them to try to sort out: far better to present it in terms of information and response, if you can.

During the match, information is also available, but all too often it doesn't reach the TDM. Let me repeat what I said before. All too often players come off bewailing the fact that they didn't get the ball against a weak opponent when in fact they never asked for it. When they do communicate, it helps if they too process the information: rather than saying 'he's slow on the turn', say 'chip it in behind him'.

Communication within rugby teams is almost uniformly bad. You hear moans, but not hard information. Yet getting good information to your TDM can shape victory. It's worthwhile actually deputing information-gathering tasks to particular people. For example, the fullback or the blind-side wing can tell immediately the opposition start a drift defence.

The ideal forum for getting a free transfer of information is the team discussion. There are few ways of spending team time that give such a return in terms of resolving problems and laying plans. The model suggested in *Total Rugby*, starting with the fullback, getting his concerns out in the open, giving him a point to think about, asking what he learned, and so through the team to end up with the captain, is the best I know. I've come to see that the method may intimidate coaches who fear that problems will be raised to which they have no adequate answers. But if it's handled as a discussion among the players concerned, that takes the load off the coach; and, like the players, once it's a regular feature it gets much easier. It is a superb way of making progress fast, and identifying real problems to be dealt with in the practices.

Part Four

The quest for space

Glenn Metcalfe, the attacking fullback

Glenn is also an attacking and defending wing – typifying the interchangability of back-three mini-team members, who constantly cover each other. All three are ideal extra men in attack, and – just as important – in defence. They exemplify the future of back-play, the players equipped with a wider range of quality skills for a flexible range of roles.

He's a product of far more demanding NZ coaches and a rugby-oriented culture. Its standards are those that this book continually advocates, and I'm happy to say that this book has made some contribution to their coaching aims and methods. Read it seriously, constantly relating it to yourself and your players, as has happened across the Southern Hemisphere.

7 The value of space

We all treasure moments of enterprise in rugby. There was that memorable moment when the All Blacks won a ruck close to their left touch, only a few metres from the opposing goal-line. Grant Battie nipped in, seized the ball, and punted it with beautiful accuracy into the arms of the New Zealand right wing, Brian Williams, alone in space on the far side of the pitch. This is a superb example of what coaches and tacticians spend much time thinking about: space that the team can attack effectively. It isn't, of course, typical: most coaches are more concerned with probabilities than with exceptional opportunities.

The case in point was an example of individual alertness by two players of great flair and initiative: it's extremely doubtful that coaching entered into it. But it focuses our attention on the need to make our tacticians and teams aware of where space is likely to be found, and to organise our team to exploit it.

Space is like a door in the wall of defence: we need to locate it, and be able to get through it. There are times when the TDM will spot space that we're not equipped to exploit, and he has to settle for a less ambitious initiative. There are times when the team may think it best to concentrate on battering a hole in the wall, feeling that if they do, the wall will collapse. There are times for all teams when such an effort is justified – providing good ball, sucking more opponents in, sapping their energy. The team that can do both is the team the good coach is aiming for.

Space is built into rugby by the laws of the game. Tactical points – scrums, line-outs, mauls – concentrate perhaps 20 players in a small space, leaving 90% of the ground to the remaining 10. By keeping its pack together as a compact threat, the team can extend this advantage to kick-offs, 22s, penalties and short line-outs. This is an elementary example of how we can create – or preserve – space.

But the coach can go much further in making his team and TDMs aware of where space is to be found, and can organise his team to exploit it. He can build an enterprising use of space into his team strategy and tactics.

How he can do this is considered below under three headings:

1. general properties of space on the pitch;

2. how the coach exploits space in a situation; and

3. how the coach equips his players to exploit the space and time available to them.

SPACE ON THE PITCH

The first thing for the coach and tactician to recognise is that not all space is equally valuable. This is very obvious in the case of the metre that takes you across the goal-line, and the metre that takes you across the half-way line.

It means, of course, that we must give concentrated attention to situations close to the goal-line – that we work out exactly how our team is best equipped to exploit them, and if necessary extend the repertoire to make absolutely sure. Equally, it demands attention to defence. This is exactly the kind of preparation for which 'three-minute rugby' is designed.

It also means that, unless we've a clear advantage in power, we shouldn't grind our way at a high cost in energy over ground that isn't intrinsically valuable. For that ground we need to carry the ball down empty channels, or kick it into space where we can hope to regain possession or force the defence to put it into touch. Our kicking must be precise – it's the kind of activity that coaching can rapidly improve – and from as close to the attacking channel as possible.

The same kind of thinking applies to lateral space. We need to examine these points in selecting our tactical situations, and incorporate them in tactical sequences so that we can exploit their possibilities fully.

Split fields give better odds

If we can introduce an extra man, a split field (i.e. a scrum, maul or ruck, with adequate space on either side) will give us better odds, for example 2 v 1 or 3 v 2 rather than 5 v 4. And remember, isolated defenders are weak.

Split fields give greater variety of attack

Without a workable blind-side, our handling attack can only be to the open, and we lose the advantage of defensive uncertainty.

Split fields with assured possession allow unorthodox formations

While this is a difference in degree – for, as you'll see, there are various ways of using a wide field – there seems to be a greater variety of such possibilities at a split field (see, for example, Fig. 12).

The implication of these points is that we need to concentrate attention on the possibility, for our particular team, of engineering such situations, but more especially on our being able to use their advantages when they present themselves.

There are also two provisos about split fields:

Narrow blind-sides are easy to defend

Within your practices, it pays to establish how much space you actually need for a given attack. A lot of ball is wasted by attacking where there is inadequate space: when in doubt, don't.

There's an optimum number of attackers for a given space

You can have too many players to work efficiently, not simply because they are cramped, but because they may become confused on the most effective choice of action. What we want in a handling attack is a high space/player ratio.

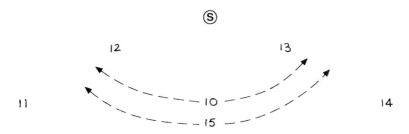

Fig. 12 Split field formation
Both 10 and 15 are available to strike on either side. 12 and 13 are standing pivots – but I have seen one glorious try when the entire defence poured out beyond 13 to cover the gap, and 13 ran 40m to score.

There are two further points to be considered in planning attacks:

Space in front of a defence is a limited advantage

In a 1 v 1 situation, space before you reach the defender can be an advantage: it lets you set him up. Again, space in front of a defence lets you move the ball wide without undue pressure. But that space takes time to cover, and gives them time to organise. If they choose not to pressurise but to shift sideways they can block your intended area of strike. If you haven't established an advantage before you reach the actual tackle line, the space has worked against you. The implication of this is that you must encourage your tactician to look at the opposition defensive tactics, and equip him with methods of turning it to advantage.

The further away from us our intended strike is, the more efficient we must be

Space and time must work together to the advantage of the attackers. If Battie's kick had been a high hanging lob, the time it took would have given the defenders time to fill the space. If we need to lie very deep to pass the ball wide, our attackers have to run further to reach the gain line, and that gives the opposing cover time to get across. Space remains space only if we can get into it faster than our opponents.

The message for the coach is plain: he must exercise quality control throughout his practices. The easiest way to reinforce this is to have fixed, objective targets. When your kicker kicks, it's got to be to a particular point, and the player for whom he's kicking has got to arrive at the same time as the ball. In passing, you can establish set standards: 'Last run we moved the ball to that point in that time . . . can we move it further faster?' You can employ reserves to count paces carrying the ball for each of your active players: 'Inside centre carried it three paces before he got it away . . . let's get down to two,' and so on. But the true core of coaching is showing him *how* to do it.

We can now turn to examine various categories of space, how we can use them, and how we can create them.

Wide field

(a) Spin the ball wide to stretch the opposing pressure and cover defence

If we can move the ball far and fast on each pass – literally spinning the ball – we can open up gaps which help to isolate defenders and give talented runners the maximum chance to beat their individual opponent. It also imposes a strain on the opposing cover. If we can retain possession at each tactical point and sustain the same form of attack, we can run them into the ground.

A team basing its attack on the speed and skill of its backs may be expected to operate in this fashion, with a single miss or double miss as a staple element in its play. It will then probably be faced with a drift defence, and it must build in a counter to it. This is best done between stand-off and inside-centre. If the inside-centre hangs back to allow the miss, and the stand-off slightly delays his pass, it forces the opposing stand-off to commit himself to one or the other. This allows either a break by the stand-off, followed by personal decision-making, or a pass to inside-centre accelerating from deep. Very often the blind-side wing can supply variety or distraction in this move.

(b) Preserve space for attack wide

Instead of seeking to move the ball wide, we concentrate on preserving space outside our winger. We can do this in two ways:

- *we adopt a very tight formation* – we can do this typically from a scrum near touch, or from a prearranged maul from a throw over the top of a short line. The backs line up close so that the ball can reach the winger either with a double miss or even in a single spin-pass from stand-off. This gives a very fast wing the maximum chance to use his speed, or to hold the ball for both centres and fullback to attack wide;

- *the wing moves back inside to preserve space wide* – we can do this typically from a line-out. The object is to get the ball wide fast, but with the line not running fast. Then either the outside-centre does a dummy switch with the winger, and is joined on the outside by the inside-centre running fast and the fullback, or the winger brings the ball back in and the same move is worked. From a short line, a very effective variation is for the ball to be taken wide by the flankers who have moved fast from their normal short line position behind the stand-off.

Split field: unorthodox back formations

From any situation in which we are moderately sure of getting the ball, we can create space for ourselves by using unorthodox formations in the backs. The aim of this is to force the opposition to commit themselves, and then to have a variety of attacks planned to take advantage of their greatest weakness. This is a basic game strategy. You can see it clearly in the kind of conjuring trick that will amuse your son. Ask him to choose a number between say, 1 and 5. You then direct him to the bookcase. If he's chosen 3, you tell him to count up to the third shelf. Then along to the third book. Then turn to the third (or thirty-third, or three hundred and thirty-third) page. Sure enough, there he'll find a note saying: 'I knew you'd choose 3.' Of course, you've also prepared similar notes for his other possible choices, but you don't tell him that! What you've done is force him to commit himself, and then turn his choice to advantage. You can do the same in rugby.

We've had considerable success by grouping stand-off, one centre, and the fullback behind the scrum, leaving one centre and wing on one side, and the other wing far out on the touch on the other side. Another very successful formation is to put one centre and wing on each side, with the stand-off and fullback slightly behind them, one on either side of the scrum.

Split field: clearing space for back-row attack

From any split-field scrum we can use the back formation to create space for a back-row attack.

Very often you see attempted back-row attacks fail because they run straight into the opposing front three. Sometimes, of course, there is method in this: you feel that you can take out an opposing back, tuck him safely away in the maul, keep possession and run against a depleted back division. Sometimes, you are counting on the known fragility of a stand-off's defence. But you can gain great advantage if you arrange for there to be no backs to interfere. For example, you can do this by putting all your backs except the right wing on the left of a midfield scrum, and your right wing out wide, or vice versa. You can enhance this by intelligent movement in the backs immediately before the GO.

You will see that the unorthodox back formations and clearing space for back-row attack are complementary, and afford a wider choice of options (see Figs 13a and 13b).

SPACE AT THE BACK

The lowest ratio of defenders to space is always at the back, where at best there'll be a fullback supported by two wingers.

The space they have to defend increases as they invade our half, and decreases as they retreat towards their line.

The number of defenders is reduced as the ball moves wide, and the wing has to come up; and at the same time the space is increased as the front three come forward.

We attack this space by kicking, and it's a measure of its importance that, even in the most committed of total rugby teams, the stand-off will kick about 40% of the ball that reaches him. It's evident from the points already made that kicking from centre is also potentially very damaging. Territorial kicking can establish us in the opposing half, which is the most comfortable place from which to attack or defend, and offers the possibility of penalty kicks at goal.

Moreover, kicking is the simplest way of getting the ball over the gain-line where our forwards can chase it. It's the standard alternative decision when things go wrong. And it's the personal skill that it's easiest for the stand-off to employ. The coach has to establish a balance appropriate to the team's designed strengths, and impose real quality control on kicking practice.

Kicking in attack has one great negative imperative: never make them a present of the ball by putting it where they can counter-attack or find a long touch. It is equally a gift of the ball if we put it into touch when they are moderately sure of winning their own throw. We kick to a point where we can directly challenge for the ball, and where, if they get it, they'll settle for a weak touch.

The stronger the wind behind us, the easier the situation becomes, since we can kick long and they can only kick short. But the great aim is to create problems for them rather than simply – unless we feel we can win their throw – make ground. Ideally, we make them turn and go back for the ball, either very close to touch, or absolutely in midfield, under organised pressure. We keep the ball in play, and force them to deal with it under difficulties.

As far as possible, it pays to kick forward rather than across. In terms of strategic channels, it's best to kick into them from their edge. That maximises accuracy and minimises reaction time. It also potentially maximises range, though that may well be secondary in attack to accuracy: the great aim is to have at least one attacker approaching the drop area as the ball arrives.

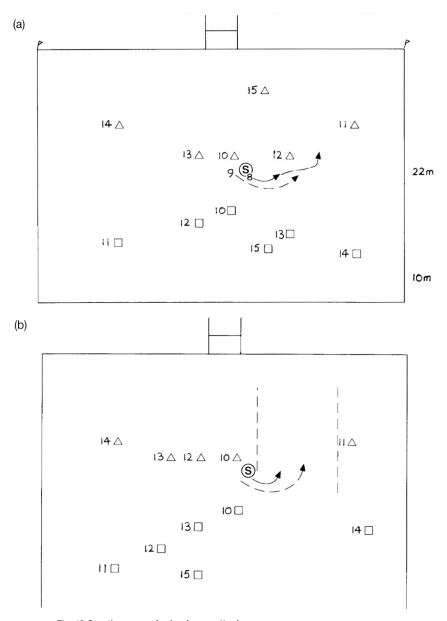

Fig. 13 Creating space for back-row attack
(a) No channel – though it would be easy to develop an attack
(b) With a channel. By shifting three players (13, 14 and 15) they have made it much more likely that the back-row attack will go forward into space.

The trouble with kicking is that it is often very badly done: it requires the same judgement, the same decision, the same level of skill, and the same organised team effort as any other form of attack if it is to be consistently successful. Kicking that relies on the opposition to make mistakes – unless you have evidence that they will – is uneconomic. At its best kicking is an essential element in a varied repertoire.

Here are two simple examples of the application of these ideas:

(i) the weakest member of the back three is the blind-side winger in a wide blind-side: if he lies up, we can move our fullback open (which tempts their fullback into midfield), and chip into the box; if he lies back, we feed from No. 8 and spin a long pass to our winger, or perhaps even get an extra man into the space;

(ii) from a line-out we can move the ball wide, and the opposing open-side winger has to come up in defence. If we have an extra man, it tempts the opposing fullback to come up shallower. When the ball reaches outside-centre we have the option: handle, if it's on; kick deep down (but not over) the touch-line, if it's not. A good kick (i.e. one that has been practised) forces the fullback to go back, covered and pressurised by three of our players. Either way, we gain.

EXAMINING SPACE AT A TACTICAL POINT

Both the coach and the TDM have to examine space at tactical points – the situations most likely to arise in the match. The coach's examination is, of course, much more leisurely and thoughtful, and has to lay the foundation for the player's examination. He is looking to see what might be done. The player is checking expectations which have been established for him.

If we take the same tactical point that we've already looked at – a scrum, our put-in, about the opposing 22m line, on the 15m line, with the blind-side on our right – we can look at the questions the coach might ask.

It's clear why he is interested in this situation. It is likely to occur: any infringement on the opposing throw is likely to give us a scrum with a 15m blind-side. It's a situation where we are almost certain to get the ball. It's fairly critical: having got so near, we should score. It is clearly defined by lines on the pitch, and is a good reference point for what can be done there or thereabouts. So in essence this space is interesting: it deserves attention. (Though it's not our concern immediately, it's also interesting because it contains an isolated defender, the left wing, and he has two duties – to cover a possible chip to the corner, or a running attack by our right wing.) We can arrange the coach's questions in four groups.

1. Interesting spaces

Where can we focus attack?

He's looking objectively, and he'd like to consider at least two possible foci of attack, since against particular opponents either might be difficult: obviously blind; less obviously wide on the left (and setting up one might distract attention and opponents from the other: he thinks of the opposing fullback).

Where can we focus attack?

He looks first at the blind and he's trying to determine the kinds of attack that might be effective. It's quite likely that angles of run come into his mind: the point is too far out to allow any running across as might happen near the line, and there's a limit on how many players can get into it.

Can we create more space by our positioning?

We can move our wing out to touch, and use whatever space his opponent leaves. We might move him across behind the scrum as a potential threat on the open, and use whichever space his opponent leaves unattended. (And the coach is perhaps considering what could be done if the scrum were another 5m into the field.)

2. How can we use our players effectively in that space?

- If we attack blind, the further *forward* we start the better: if we start deep, they can close up the space before we arrive.

- If we want to accelerate the attack, we need the striker – the eventual ball-carrier – to be moving fast, which means coming from *deeper*.

- And we'll need to get him *wide* enough to be reasonably clear of their back row.

- To *preserve* that space, we need someone to check their flanker.

- And our striker has to *run straight*, so we want him moving wide early. This will help *preserve space* outside him, and keep passes possible both in and out.

3. How do we arrange support?

- How far do we want to organise our action? Not too far: if we can get our striker running straight in space, we can expect the lads to improvise more satis-factorily than we can organise.

- Where do we want support? On the inside, since if the striker is tackled it'll be almost certainly from the inside, and that's how he'll rotate. There is one plus in using the right flanker: he's there. But there are two minuses: he mustn't move till the ball-carrier is ahead of him (if he moves forward before that he delays offering support), and he has a very limited acceleration zone. He can be useful as a standing receiver, immediately shifting the ball to the No. 8 or left flanker coming round.

The No. 8 is running from a little deeper, and is almost immediately in a support position. If he gives the pass, and then moves across before driving forward, he should be able to add punch to the move.

- And that would allow the right flanker to come across behind to cover if things go wrong and to be ready for a rollback if the striker is caught.

4. How about timing?

The only problems are:

- getting the scrum-half wide and deep fast before No. 8 breaks;
- getting the right flanker to stay down till scrum-half is past him;
- getting the right wing to time his run – and timing is the next thing we'll look at.

Of course, this is a simplified account: we want to concentrate on space, so we're not worrying about wheeling packs, and not taking in possibilities like a chip to the corner (if their winger is up flat), or a kick from scrum-half up high on the posts. These are all perfectly valid if your players have ability, and they too would involve considerations of space – the winger out on touch for the first, to keep the ball in play; the centres and stand-off up flatter to pressurise midfield defence in the second – but not in as much detail. But it's useful in illustrating the way in which considerations of space influence the coach's thinking and help him set up the start with a better chance of success.

THE COACH AND TIMING AT A TACTICAL POINT

Now even if we manage to get players running in the right direction, in space, at a satisfactory speed, it's useless if their arrival doesn't coincide with the ball. If it doesn't they have to slow down, run flatter, stop (to avoid getting offside); and if it arrives too early they get it well back from the gain-line and their chances are limited. It's exactly what you see from a stand-off who doesn't know that he *starts* to run when the scrum-half puts his hands on the ball (or more accurately, when he sees the ball in the scrum-half's hands), or a centre doing the same thing off a standing stand-off.

What do we need in order to be able to control timing to co-ordinate more complex starts?

Well, it's all very easy once you've seen it:

(i) we need to know the ball is immediately available to the scrum-half;

(ii) we need to know how long in this particular match the forwards can safely expect to hold it available;

(iii) as soon as the scrum-half is sure of (i) he can signal to the backs, and they can start moving into position;

(iv) the ball is given to the scrum-half only when and immediately he calls for it. He calls for it *at the moment determined in practice of the start*, usually when he sees the stand-off (or receiver – it might be a centre, a winger, a fullback, a flanker running off a maul) reach a particular point. This means that he is never under pressure: he can part with the ball immediately he receives it.

Each of these points has implications. The first is the need to get the ball to the back, under control, of every scrum, maul and ruck. Where possible – for example in the maul – the forward holding the ball should be looking at the scrum-half, ready to feed him. In scrum and ruck the rearmost player(s) must hold the ball with knees or feet, ready to release it as soon as the tap on his/their leg is felt.

If, in a given game, the opposition pressure is too great to allow holding the ball, it immediately limits you to actions that can be done quickly, and may force you to simplify your game drastically – but that's an extreme case. Usually, you can expect to be able to hold the ball for at least the few moments that let you organise your attack. Another limitation is that under pressure you can rarely afford to let a forward drop out of the scrum early, though his absence is less critical at maul and ruck.

The signal for back movement is visual: once the scrum-half knows the ball is immediately available he slaps his leg. He watches them move into their new positions, and at a moment determined by trial and error in practices calls for the ball. Once it's in his hands, everything clicks into position as it does when no extraneous timing is needed.

An obvious example is the fullback, who may normally have difficulties in joining the line at speed if they are moving fast. Now it's easy: at the scrum-half's 'ball available' signal, he sets off, and the scrum-half spins the ball so that it reaches him via the three-quarters just as he hits the line. Another obvious example is the forward who is going to take the ball on from the maul: he drops out and waits for the signal. He can then set off on the signal, either side of the maul, running for space, confident that the ball will be given to him when he wants it.

If we take a simple case of this timing at work, you'll understand it very easily. Consider the case used above in discussion about space (the scrum with a blind-side on the right), with the scrum maybe five metres further into the field of play. We can look at quite an effective and very simple move: the stand-off switching sides to attack the blind (see Fig. 14 a, b and c).

It was pointed out under 'space' that it's futile starting the run from deep: you immediately become a target, and may have to carry the ball from 15m behind the gain-line, while the opposing back row sharpen their teeth and come forward to catch you behind your back row. This is not a good situation.

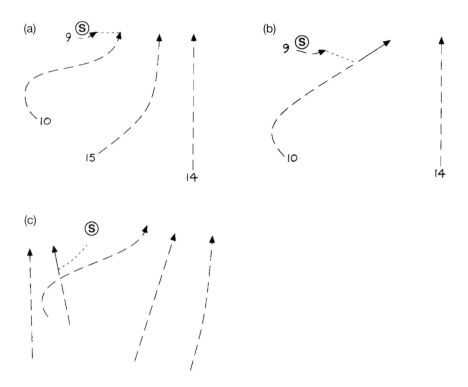

Fig 14 Typical use of controlled timing
(a) Typical attack to blind using timing device. 9 does just enough to check blind flanker. 9 has three different possible receivers. Where does he look?
(b) Typical attack when 10 is quick, and has opened up space on the right. Again the time device is used, with 9 doing just enough to check left flanker.
(c) Alternative when 10's strike into the blind has been used, and his movement displaces 10 in defence. 15 runs as stand-off at moment established in practice, with 12, to fork their 13. 10 runs flat to stay onside. Why is it more effective against split centres?

However, if you simply start running, looking for a short pass, almost flat with the back of the scrum, minimising the back row's reaction time, you may find yourself having to slow dramatically because the ball isn't there.

If we use the timing arrangement, life becomes easy, or at least easier. You're in your normal start position, your chest and shoulders indicating your intention to move the ball open. When the 'ball available' signal comes, you take a couple of steps open to get your immediate opponent moving open, then swing fast back to the blind. In practice, you've perfected the timing of the scrum-half's call for the ball, and his pass. So he gives it to you precisely where you want it.

In practice, of course, you will also have looked at the kind of advantages you can derive from intelligent use of space. This may affect the line on which you run. I've seen this move performed with a very swift stand-off running on a straight line across the face of the flanker, and on into space: another swings out at the start to let him straighten as he runs on to the ball, checking the flanker for the swerve that follows. The great thing is that you should be aware of the possibility of choice, and choose what suits you.

In this start only one timing is needed. It's possible, though, and completely practicable, to arrange a two-step timing.

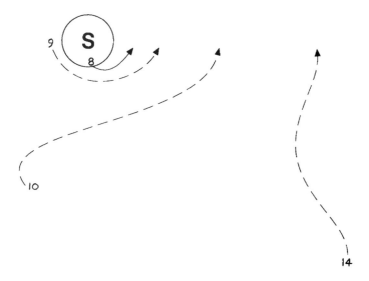

Fig. 15 **Exploiting the same channel using both timing devices**
As soon as the ball is available, the signal is given and 10 and 14 start their run into position. Seconds later, at a time established in practice, 8 breaks, feeds 9, and a combined attack is underway.

Let's put our two moves together to illustrate the possibilities. The scrum is now just to the right of midfield. We've moved both our centres to the left, and our winger has moved out to the right touch-line. We've created a great deal of space. Our full-back has moved out to the left as an additional threat, to keep their fullback away.

We're going to open with the No. 8 breaking to set the scrum-half up, and we're going to bring an unexpected extra man and a change of pace to the move by having the stand-off turn up on the outside of the scrum-half.

How are we going to arrange the timing? We already need timing for the first part of the move, to let the scrum-half get wide and deeper before the No. 8 goes. We'd like to see him functioning like a local stand-off, ready and balanced to make the most of the No. 8's pass.

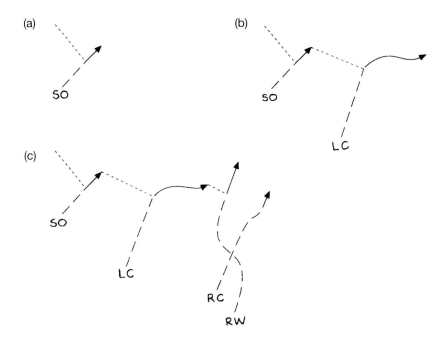

***Fig 16* Bringing a player in from deep**

Rather than simply showing how to bring in a fullback, here's a start using the open wing, who will swing in-between the centres to take the ball on the burst from first centre.

(a) On the call the SH puts the ball closer to SO so that he runs slowly on to it

(b) SO puts the ball back to LC who has started off a little deep and is running at some pace as SO. Then LC swings flat across field: the longer he can hold the ball, the more margin there is for error; and the flatter he runs, the longer he can hold the ball

(c) RC is lying a little wider than usual and when LC turns out, he too swings away to create space for RW. RW starts as normal but swings on to his strike course as established in practice. LC still has the option of giving it straight out to RC

Now you work out how to get the fullback running outside the right centre

Solution: If we use the timing device, and start fullback and RW before the rest, we can operate the whole start at speed using normal positions and flat passes. It's still better to have LC ready to run across, though, to provide a margin for safety.

To do this there has to be a pause between the scrum-half hitting the No. 8 to tell him to start, and the No. 8's break. You can do this in two ways. The first is when the No. 8 can twist to see him, as he might if he were feeding the ball. Then he waits till he sees him check, and immediately goes. The second is equally simple: at the signal he starts to count (1,000 . . . 2,000 . . . equivalent to one second, two seconds), and at a number established in practice he gets his head up and goes.

How about the stand-off? He needs enough time to get into a precise position outside the scrum-half, running fast and straight. This means exaggerating the curve suggested in the second case above: he has to make a fair amount of ground.

Once again there are two ways of doing it. In the first we simply adjust the No. 8's count to tie in with the stand-off rather than the scrum-half. This has the disadvantage of having the scrum-half out in space for a moment, clearly visible to the flanker. In practice, however, it works adequately.

A little more difficult, but avoiding that particular disadvantage, is method two. In this, the scrum-half signals to the stand-off as soon as the ball is available, waits until he sees him reach a point on his run determined in practice, slaps the No. 8, and gets out into position. The No. 8 does the scrum-half count, and goes.

I'm very pleased with this little device: it's thoroughly practicable, and it extends the range of what we can do. It is also, of course, a good example of a tactical call by the stand-off. He sees the position, creates space by keeping the centres and the wing out of the way, sets up the move, and the team executes it with a fine precision impossible without central control.

8 **Defining the run**

SPACE, TIME AND THE PLAYER

We can identify four factors in a player's support positioning/running which we can set out to improve.

1. *Width* – is his lateral spacing from the ball-carrier appropriate?
2. *Depth* – is his distance behind the ball-carrier appropriate?
3. *Direction* – is his line of running appropriate?
4. *Speed* – is his speed appropriate?

We can assess all of these in terms of a contribution to the immediate team objective.

At any moment, we expect an effective compromise. The factor that – once the technical objectives are understood – most influences the quality of the compromise is time. How much time the player has available depends on:

- *the speed with which he makes his decision and acts on it* – if he starts half a second early it will give him an advantage of perhaps three metres in the support area. The coach must encourage continuous assessment (see page 70), and positive action (see for example, page 46);

- *the speed with which he moves on an effective line* – he has to start fast as well as quickly: the first half dozen strides are extremely important. Start fast; arrive in balance, and able to choose direction and speed. The coach prescribes speed work, and monitors performance;

- *the time available at particular situations* – for the backs, first phase offers adequate time to get into established positions, but it's harder in second phase. Width and especially depth may be sacrificed, and result in gross difficulties in direction and speed when the movement starts. The coach demands discipline: get into position, *then* take a breather;

- *the time created by an early call* – any delay in the call makes it difficult to get into position, or rehearse mentally what's going to happen. The coach has to encourage constant assessment of the developing situation, and early calls in all practices. He should also check that communication to backs and forwards is working;

- *the time created by a controlled release of the ball* – in general, the ball should never be released from the pack till the scrum-half calls for it, and he should never call for it until he knows how it's going to be used. The coach keeps asking for this in practices. More specifically, a controlled release of the ball as described above (see for example, page 78) allows shifts of position to take place with a guarantee of accurate timing. Of course, the long-term aim is to reduce the delay to zero, especially if the attack has gathered momentum.

The scrum-half can control the whole tempo of operations – within the limits of the pack's ability to hold the ball – and so calm things down when the team are edgy and speed them up when the team's humming.

ESTABLISHING CRITERIA OF SUCCESS

If we examine the first four conditions we can easily sort out basic aims in each.

1. Width

OTHER THINGS BEING EQUAL, IT PAYS TO BE WIDE RATHER THAN CLOSE

- It makes the passer's task much easier, by making the timing of the pass less critical. In a normal 2 v 1, good timing means giving the pass when the defender is committed to the ball-carrier but before the ball-carrier is under pressure. This happens – for all practical purposes – as soon as the ball-carrier is closer to the defender than to the receiver. If the receiver is very close, then the ball-carrier has to get uncomfortably close to the defender before passing.
- It makes it much harder for the defender to catch the receiver.
- It forces the cover to go that little bit further.
- It allows us to exploit spin passing more fully – an increasingly important consideration against supplemented defences.

2. Depth

OTHER THINGS BEING EQUAL, IT PAYS TO TAKE THE BALL FLAT RATHER THAN BACK

Every time the ball goes back it creates time for the defence to get across. If it goes back a metre, it gets them about a metre further across.

This is true for the individual defender in the 2 v 1, and it's true for the whole pack and industrious backs covering against the opposing back division. If you pass back, you're making a gift of time to the defenders.

Of course, being up to take the flat-pass doesn't mean being there before the ball arrives. The ball-carrier should always be able to pass flat to space. He should never have to pass *at* his supporter, always flat *in front of him*. And the receiver must reach that point running at the speed he wants.

Taking width and depth together, then, we can say that other things being equal we're looking for the player to turn up comfortably wide running on to a flat-pass. This provides a basic criterion for all of our intensive handling practices, and as coaches we've got to encourage and insist on quality control in this respect by our players.

Clearly, the built-in 'other things being equal' rule applies to the match context. The width may be dictated by where the space into which the receiver intends to run is located; the depth may be dictated by the pressure of a flat defence. When we say 'flat' we mean 'as flat as practicable': you cannot hope to move the ball wide if you don't allow yourselves adequate depth to start with.

3. Direction of run as ball-carrier or potential ball-carrier

The receiver can reach the point defined above running in any direction, but only a few of those directions will let him contribute effectively to the team objectives. At its worst, he may reach that point, running flat across the pitch. In first phase, however, it's easy for the coach to establish the back positionings that allow the player to choose his exact line of run (see below); and in loose play he can always encourage his players to use the time available as fully as possible, to help in that choice.

> *OTHER THINGS BEING EQUAL, THE BEST DIRECTION IS STRAIGHT UPFIELD*

In other words, though for particular purposes we may diverge from that line, the sooner – as ball-carrier or potential ball-carrier – we get back to it the better. This is because:

- it preserves space outside – the channel is kept clear for the ball-carrier or his supporter on the outside;

- it makes it easier for his supporter coming across on the inside;

- it checks his immediate opponent, and may make him more vulnerable to evasion;

- it checks the cover;

- it minimises the danger of being caught far behind the gain line where it's difficult to cover a counter-attack.

But none of this is a licence to run straight into an opponent: the overriding priority is to keep the ball moving forward into space. And one exception is so important it deserves consideration here: if you intend to pass, it's a great help not to be running straight; that can block your hips, and destroy the rhythm of your pass.

4. Speed

> *OTHER THINGS BEING EQUAL, THE HIGHER*
> *YOUR SPEED THE BETTER*

The higher your speed:

- the less time it allows the cover to get across;
- the more critical timing is for the immediate opponent;
- the more chance there is he'll lose his resolution;
- the more likely it is that you'll be able to drive through the tackle at least for that vital metre or two that makes life easy for your support and may let you get the ball away;
- the less likely it is that you'll get caught behind the gain-line.

There are, of course, exceptions to this as to every rule. You may benefit from running slowly if it creates the chance to change pace either personally or as a unit, and, as we'll see below, you'll benefit if it allows you to defer a decision until the opposition have committed themselves.

Reaching an effective compromise

To turn up at precisely the right point, running on precisely the right line, at precisely the right speed is certainly possible – for a centre, say, from a scrum. But most players, most of the time, are producing compromises, because too many conditions are outside their control. If they had time, they could do it – and we must learn to make the most of the time available to us – but usually they have to choose between direction and speed. The centre crabbing sideways is a case in point: he didn't get wide enough or deep enough, fast enough; the flanker who tums up inside the wing, running on a line that prevents him from doing anything useful, has sacrificed direction to speed.

The coach's job is to arrange the best possible compromise over a range of such cases, sometimes by precise positioning, often by encouraging speed of decision and action.

PUTTING THE PRINCIPLES INTO PRACTICE

These principles are going to find expression within all our strategies and tactics. We employ them in examining and setting up situations. They are also central to getting our backs functioning effectively as a unit. What follows is a discussion of how we set about putting them into practice, starting with this last purpose. It's an edited version of an actual discussion with a prominent player thinking of becoming a coach.

Do you think it's important that the backs should function as a unit?
Yes. Team play is based on co-operation: you'd think it ridiculous if individual forwards didn't function as part of the pack, wouldn't you? And you know that even a pack which has grown together, so that their sense of how they're going to play is strong, can benefit from intelligent leadership? Well that's exactly true of the backs. It's a way of maximising your advantage by having the backs co-operate for a specific purpose which is appropriate at that moment, rather than letting each one explore for himself.

Doesn't that interfere with individual freedom in the backs?
Yes, but no more than 'every man for himself' does. A centre's liberty is a winger's wasted afternoon. Central control means that everyone should be presented with a better chance to show what he can do – if it's working well, a tailor-made chance, with maximum support.

But what if chances present themselves unexpectedly?
Everyone has a right to back his own judgement, and if it works, great. If he keeps doing it and he's wrong, you have a selection problem.

So it shouldn't handicap the flair of the players . . . ?
This kind of control ensures that the flair has a chance to show itself. The flair is built into the planning. You organise to give the player of flair the best chance to show what he can do.

Isn't that going to be a long-term policy?
Yes. Short term you should see gains, if only by bringing your best strikers into operation, but consistent success means long-term planning and preparation.

How long does it take to establish a policy like that?
It probably depends on how well the players know you at the start. If they know you and trust you, by the end of the season I'd expect to see some kind of organic growth.

Would you like to describe how you set up a back division?
In terms of being able to get the ball quickly and consistently to a player running on a given line at a given speed?

Yes. For example, since you wrote Total Rugby, there's been a debate about whether the stand-off should run on to the ball or take it standing still.
Well, if you've the know-how you can get him running on to the ball and passing it on at any point you wish – the same point for example, that you might choose for him to stand at. If he runs; he's a potential striker, a potential distraction for the opposing back row; if he stands still, he isn't. So I think he should run.

So you'd never have him standing?
Never say 'never' . . . sorry: in games it's rarely wise to say 'never' or 'always'. If you have your stand-off just standing there you could use him for a pivot, with the ball being fed to whoever is running into space. Or you could use him as a relay station: he can throw out extremely long and, with practice, accurate passes, and shift the focus of attack very fast from one side of the ground to the other.

But I'd really think of these as exceptions rather than the rule. Where you find a stand-off standing, it means, as a rule, that they haven't developed the expertise to get him passing the ball at that point while on the run.

I suppose my own feeling is that I'd like my players to be able to cope with as many situations and potentialities as possible – the more flexible and adaptable they are, the better our chances.

Obviously, though, the New Zealanders wouldn't agree with you.
Well, you have the choice of two package deals: the New Zealand one; and the standard one, which, incidentally, many New Zealand coaches still favour. The New Zealand one has the outstanding advantage of all NZ rugby – simplicity. Because of the power and athleticism of their forwards, and fitness beyond anything we've imagined here, they're able to impose their simple structured rugby on the opposition. There's not much to go wrong with it if they get the edge up front. The same's true of their half-back play.

The NZ half-back deal often features a standing stand-off. You can see the simplicity of that: it gives a standing target, and it guarantees the rest of the line begins to operate at a set depth. And there's a pay-off for the scrum-half too. If you watch them, you'll see they've got their lead leg on the line of pass before they touch the ball. All their weight is on the back foot, of course, and from there they sweep the ball away without foot movement. They still manage to block and they still manage to pick it up, though.[1]

---

1. While I was coaching in Spain in 1991, an All Black scrum-half (whom I had actually coached as a schoolboy in New Zealand) travelled down to see me; he *did* block, because of imbalance, and his pass suffered because of it. A general point: the most talented players are those for whom coaching is most important.

So what's the problem?
Well, both packages are based on trade-offs – you're buying one strength at the cost of other weaknesses. The New Zealanders pay for simplicity by renouncing their first five-eighth as an attacker. Of course, even then, he's got some value: you can't just ignore him. And at scrum-half, you're depending on getting decent ball coming to your back foot; you'd look odd trying to adjust your position to a bobbling ball. But they presumably don't stick their foot out till they're sure.

And you think these points outweigh the simplicity?
As I say, I'd like my players to be able to do both. I mean, you've got to arrange for any stand-off to take the ball standing for particular purposes – well, maybe not standing – he wants the ball just in front of him, for example, so that he moves easily into his punt or drop-kick. It's merely a matter of arranging signals. As I said before, I reckon that if you can make it possible to run smoothly on to the ball, it gives you that much more power. It's a matter of coaching expertise and player discipline. And on principle, I don't think we should go overboard about fashion. One year it's all French lines of running, the next it's New Zealand five-eighths – but really it's lack of domestic coaching expertise.

OK. Let's say we'll stick with the standard method. Are there any points about how the stand-off should position himself?
The great thing is to get to his starting point fast and accurately. That's especially important in second phase, where the great temptation is to be too far forward, which automatically cuts down your options in the backs. He needs to be physically in balance – feet normally close, if anything outside foot forward, so he can view the scrum-half easily. He's got to be at ease physically and emotionally, and in fine focus mentally.

What exactly is he concentrating on?
Before he gets there, he should have been predicting to himself what will be on. Once he's there, he needs to know what to look for – what's significant in that situation – and he depends on experience and good coaching for that. He wants to call every time, and call early. As soon as he's done that he should be figuring out what to do if he gets bad ball – where he'll kick is what it comes down to. The great thing is to use all the time available to make good decisions.

Earlier on when I asked about his position, I really meant where does he start from . . . ?
Most stand-offs operate from a spot that offers a reasonable compromise tilted in favour of the team strategy. Broadly speaking, the wider you intend to strike, the deeper you should take the ball, and vice versa: it's a matter of creating space to move the ball to get it wide, and limiting the opposition reaction time if you're running it close in. With beginners I say, go back eleven paces and out two: that's a fair position.

And how fast does he run on to the ball?
We can control that by controlling the distance ahead of him the scrum-half puts the ball. The stand-off calls for the ball he wants. For some purposes, it might be straight to his right hand for a right-footed kick virtually standing still. Quite often, he'll want to run on to the ball quite slowly (so the ball is put quite close to him) because he wants to hold the ball to let someone come into the line, or to get the opposition to commit themselves before he commits himself to a particular pass. Usually, he wants to run on to the ball quite fast but in balance – and you find how far ahead of him that pass has to be by experiment, intelligent trial and error. Just make sure that he's comfortable: run him through often enough to accustom him to a given speed before he tries it in the match. And remind the scrum-half that late in the match the stand-off may not be quite as nippy as he was early on.

So how do you set it up?
If you've got *Total Rugby* it's all in there. Still, briefly, it goes like this. Set the scrum-half up for a right-hand pass, and walk back from him on a 45 degree angle about ten strides. Then get him passing to you really accurately: it's got to reach you waist-high, dead on line. You'll find his lead leg causes most of the problems. That generally means he's off balance. Encourage him to get his rear foot closer to the ball at pick-up, and to go down bending his rear knee. Explain that, as soon as he touches the ball, he's got to whip it away – or he'll get his hands kicked off.

Then call in the stand-off. Tell him he mustn't move till he sees the scrum-half's hands on the ball. Tell him he's got to cross the line of pass to you at right-angles, just in front of you – so he knows exactly the line he's running on.

But surely taking the pass at right-angles means that the fly-half is running across?
It looks like that, I agree. But look at it this way. The point at which the stand-off takes the ball will be the same whichever angle he's running on, won't it? How many lines could you draw through that point?

As many as you like, I suppose, but only a few would be relevant to the fly-half.
That's right. Well, take a point and draw those lines. We can arrange any line of run you like – it won't move that point wider at all, will it?

No, but if you carry the line beyond it, it will.
Yes – so the problem is speed in moving the ball. If we take three strides before moving the ball and we're running at right-angles to the pass, or three strides when we're running straight, which uses up more space?

Neither's much good, is it? The straight line uses up space between the lines – between us and the opposition – and the other one space across the field.
So in both cases the critical factor is less the line of run than the speed of moving the ball?

I suppose so.
But that's possibly related to the actual running speed?

Yes, you're bound to use up more space if you're moving faster.
So we need to look at running speed and speed of passing rather than at the previous line of run?

Yes.
Well, there you are. We started talking about angle of run and we've ended up identifying a different problem. I use the right-angle line because it makes life so much easier for everyone. It makes it very easy for the scrum-half to judge how far ahead to put the ball, and it makes taking and giving far more easy for the stand-off. You've only to try it to find how much the stand-off benefits from it.

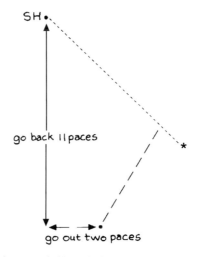

Fig 17 Setting up the scrum-half stand-off tie-up
(1) Go out to a point where you think SO will be able to run on to the ball at right-angles and get a little deeper on that line
(2) Then forget SO for a minute or two: make sure SH can hit you regularly with the ball. Tell SO to watch and judge whether he can intercept it – but he can't move till SH puts his hands on it
(3) SO knows the line of run, but he can move his start forward or go back till he's running comfortably fast on to the ball that SH is trying to get to you.
  It's that distance that you're trying to establish, and that the SH has to learn. Once he's learned it, you've got it cracked.

I suppose it stops him blocking?
There's hope for you yet! Yes, it means that his hips move easily in the pass, and that he's set up to give long passes if he needs to. As you know, I work on getting

him to straighten as he gives the pass – I stand outside his line of run so he's forced to straighten to keep inside me. If he straightens before he gives the pass, you see an immediate deterioration in his passing, and that's what happens when he runs too straight in the first place.

So the big problem's the actual ball-speed through his hands?
That's it – and you've seen the little exercises I do to improve that.

The one where you have them trotting side by side, reaching and giving so that the ball moves along the line continuously without actually being passed?
That kind of thing: you can look it up in the book.

How about running speed?
I've always aimed to get him taking the ball at about 80% of top speed – but that's done with a purpose. If we can do the difficult one well, the rest are easy. It gives us a better range, and greater flexibility: if we need to take the ball running fast we can do it; if we don't, it's simple to cut the lead to whatever's felt to be appropriate. And a simple signal will give us the ball standing still if we want it.

Don't discount running fast on to the ball. It checks their stand-off, which may seriously weaken an intended drift defence, and it checks their back row.

But the All Blacks want it standing all the time?
Well, for a long time they were keen to get their stand-off running: they felt it was a weakness in their game that they couldn't get him running on to the ball consistently. But, as I've said, there are certain advantages. You get a set target for the scrum-half, which is simple to hit. It also lets the scrum-half get his lead leg out on the line of pass before he touches the ball, and that puts him in a position where he's less likely to pick the ball up before he passes. Of course, he pays a bit in the weight shift, but perhaps that's not so important. And the great thing is that you can guarantee the depth at which the ball will start to move down the line.

But you don't do that yourself.
No. I reckon we can get a better compromise in which we keep the stand-off as a potential striker. We've got the expertise to have him running on to the ball consistently, and getting it away at the right depth.

So, if he's taking the ball moving, we come back to the question of how fast.
Yes. I've said there are advantages in speed; but there are also advantages in moving on to the ball slowly. It's another trade-off. If we can hold the ball just a little longer at stand-off by running very slowly, it forces the opposition defence to commit themselves before we commit ourselves. That's a great advantage – at least potentially: it should let him take advantage of what they're doing. But the longer he holds it, the longer he gives their cover to get across field. That again is

only potential: they may hang around to watch him. If they don't, it makes wide attack very difficult. So you've got to balance one against the other. But it's certainly a method every stand-off should be able to use, if only occasionally. It gives him another weapon.

You think we shouldn't give him a single role.
I think flexibility is a great quality: to be able to respond with a variety of possible attacks to different opportunities.

OK, can we move on to . . .
Just one last point in favour of the right-angled line. There are times when the timing of the pass from stand-off is very important – usually when he's passing to the potential striker. By running across slightly – as he will if he doesn't straighten – he can hold the ball that little bit longer, and get more precise timing of the pass. In effect, running across delays by a stride or so your meeting with your opponent.

OK – I've seen it working. What do we do next?
You tell the scrum-half he's got to get the ball to you before the stand-off can move, and you tell the stand-off that nevertheless he's going to intercept it – so where does he want to stand? Let him move back along the 90 degree line till he's happy, get them calm, then let them have a go.

What it he doesn't get to it?
Just check that he didn't slip, or start too late. If he didn't, ask him whether he wants to move forward or back along his line of run. He'll move forward, of course. He may have to move forward several times, and jockey around till he gets it right, running on comfortably fast.

What if he comes off the line of run, running out?
Again, check that he didn't slip or start too slow. If he didn't it means that he's still a little too far back from the ball. Explain to the scrum-half that if this happens in the match, he's putting the ball just a little too far ahead of his partner.

What if the stand-off has to check?
Check that he didn't start too early. If he checks or slows down, he ought in this exercise to move a little further back – he can't change the timing of his run, so he must adjust his start position. Explain to the scrum-half that if this happens in the match, he's putting the ball too close to his partner.

So by changing his start position relative to the line of pass, you're really trying to find exactly how far ahead of him the scrum-half should pass? That particular line of pass isn't the only one . . .

Dead right. Once the stand-off is comfortable running on to the ball, I'm going to move away after giving the scrum-half dozens of warnings to look at the distance between me and the stand-off and learn it.

OK I'll maybe come back to that. What about the way he catches the ball?
He doesn't 'catch it' – he welcomes it as a friend. All he has to do is to stop it going any further. He puts his outside hand, relaxed, on the line of flight – and the earlier he can do that without changing the direction of run the better – and stops it. He'll get to it earlier, and get a better sight of it, if he turns his shoulders towards the pass, and extends his arm. As soon as the inside hand makes contact, it should (if he's going to pass) be sweeping on into the pass.

That's when you have people counting the steps he takes with the ball?
Not at the start. He's got to feel very comfortable first. Once he's comfortable you can start talking about speed. But the real thing is accuracy. If he trades accuracy for speed . . . well, it just won't work: it's not fast if the next player can't take it easily and smoothly.

But after that, yes. I usually put markers down at the point at which he receives the ball, and the point by which he's got to have passed it. Then I gradually cut down the distance he carries it. Counting steps comes later, when the whole line's running. The marker is useful, too, in getting him to straighten slightly as he passes – not before, but in the act of passing.

How about if he drops it?
It's like anyone else. Check that the receiving hand and arm are relaxed – in fact that everything above the hips is relaxed. I often say: 'run from the hips down, and save everything else for the ball'. Some players get tight when they try to run fast, get more upright. It's hard then to keep your head over the ball. And, of course, 'keep your eye on the ball,' which means really looking at it; not just being conscious of a white blob, but seeing that ball right into your hands. Especially when you're trying to be fast, you sometimes turn your eyes to the receiver before you've got it.

Have you moved out of the way by this time?
Well, later rather than sooner: give the scrum-half every chance to learn the distance. Explain to him how important it is. I usually dig my heel in the turf before I go, and check later with both of them: 'Is this about right? . . . is this about right?'

And how is he going to use it?
I thought we'd . . . For different purposes the stand-off will want different starting positions. In any of these, if he wants to run on to the ball, he wants it that distance ahead of him.

Yes, I understand that, but that's not the only distance ahead of him the ball can go . . .

No. He may want it just in front of him, to let him step forward into a precise tactical kick. Get them to try it, and get the stand-off to offer a target – that far-away hand where he wants to receive the ball.

Isn't that asking a lot?

Yes, but it's in everyone's interest that you insist on top-quality standards. You're not being kind letting them away with less. Keep expecting the scrum-half to monitor his own performance, and correct his own mistakes. If it goes in front of you – you're the target – there's a reason for it (check his lead foot: is it blocking)?; if it goes high, there's a reason for it (check that he's not coming up too fast); if it's inconsistent, check that he's in balance at the end of the pass, and not putting a hand down to stop himself from falling forward. Ask him where the hand behind the ball must be going.

What about the stand-off's pass?

Make sure you're happy with the halves before you start bringing in a centre. The rest of the backs should be busy offstage, practising kicking and catching, 2 v 1s, passing back over the shoulder, touch rugby, and so on. When you call him up, let him watch two or three runs. Then:

- mark the spot where the stand-off will pass the ball;
- walk along the line of the flat pass and with the centre decide the point at which he wants to run on to the ball; mark it;
- ask him to choose his line of run – you can explain that if he expects to pass he'll do it far more efficiently running slightly out;
- walk forward from the ball-reception point on that line of run; turn and get the centre to go back behind the reception point on the same line. He'll find himself a long way from the stand-off, and that is the best guarantee that he'll always be able to choose his line of run and not be forced to run across. All he has to do to get the line right is to aim to cross the mark you made earlier;
- tell him he mustn't start moving until the stand-off starts moving, and ask him where along the line of run his starting position should be to let him run fast on to the flat-pass. Run them through it often enough to let him adjust his starting position relative to the pass, exactly as you did for the stand-off above. Check that the pass is flat. Just as there was a competition between scrum-half and stand-off, so the stand-off is trying to reveal the centre's lack of pace by spinning the ball flat across the front of him while he's still yards behind. Go out in front to check that line of run – see Fig. 18.

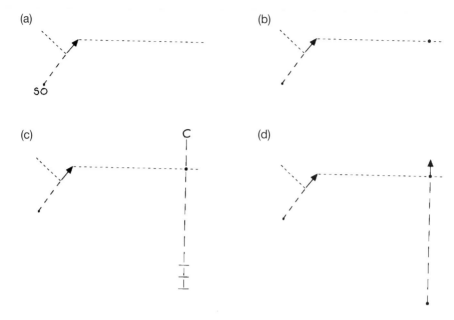

Fig 18 How to get your centres running fast on the line they want. (What does this centre intend to do?)

(a) Establish where SO will be able to pass, and the line of a flat pass

(b) Establish the point where LC wants to run on to that pass

(c) Establish the line of run that LC wants. Coach walks up that line, turns and sends LC back on the reciprocal. Coach remains where he is to act as marker, and to check accuracy of running.

Coach asks LC to start simultaneously with SO, and to guess the right start position on the line. He modifies it till it's right

(d) When he's done it successfully half-a-dozen times, he has to memorise his start position relative to SO. It'll look very odd, but it's right!

Once he's got it, make sure he uses it: build it into simple rhythms so that he recognises he's got to work to get there fast.

Any tips about the stand-off's pass?

Now he's got a clear, organised target, you can begin to ask him to pass further, by putting the centre a little further out. (Will the centre have to move his starting position further forward or further back as he moves further out?) As the pass gets longer the stand-off will find it pays to run slightly more out, and to use a spin-pass. Explain to him that for some purposes he'll need to pass a little backward of flat. Explain that whenever we intend to strike wide we should build in a miss-pass, occasionally from stand-off and occasionally from inside-centre to disguise our intention. Or a double miss, or a treble.

And then we add a second centre?
Yes. It's much slower than just pushing them out in a rough line, but once they've experienced that confident acceleration along a chosen line of run on to a flat-pass, they won't look back.

You add the second centre in exactly the same way, starting with the flat pass from inside-centre, and develop it in the same way. But try to build on success: delay calling him up till you're happy with the way the ball will reach him.

You keep emphasising this flat pass. Would you never pass back?
Remember: it means as flat as is practicable. As usual, there are times when you'll pass back because you have to: the man outside you is out of position, either because he didn't start fast or because he's weary, or because he's hanging back to escape a very high-pressure defender. And there's one clear case where you'd pass back by arrangement. What would that be?

Off the top of my head, I don't know.
You can work it out. What would it be like in terms of the stand-off?

Like putting the ball closer to him?
Exactly. And what did that do?

Let him run on to the ball more slowly.
And why did we build that in? What advantages did it create?

Well, it made it easier for us to introduce players running from deep.
That's my boy . . . and it also allows for a change of pace, if the centre reckons he can beat his man that way. But we buy these advantages at the cost of what?

You mean if he takes it running slower, it'll be easier for their cover?
There you are: it's easy, isn't it? Remember, though, that there will be matches where the cover isn't a problem. But it is easy. There's nothing esoteric about it, nothing veiled in deep mystery. You can work it out if you take time to think about it. Well, you've seen me getting kids to work it out, haven't you?

Yes . . . but you ask the right questions. It's easy then.
I suppose so, but doing the basic work isn't that hard: and it's very satisfying. It keeps you interested.

OK How often do we have to do this positional working out?
You need to get it right at the start, and it's well worthwhile polishing it before you see it deteriorate in the match. It's your quality standards that you have to impose on the players to the point where they willingly adopt them because they make playing so much more satisfying. Same with the passing: if you start off each

session with handling, make sure it's quality handling, with real control of positioning. Expect them to be great, and show them how to do it.

How do you bring in the fullback?
The big difficulty is timing. If he starts too early he sends a signal to the opposition, and he may have to slow down or check that the ball doesn't arrive as he does; if he starts too late he never catches up with the line.

There are three basic ways of coping with it:

1. get the scrum-half to put his pass close to the stand-off so that he runs slowly on to the ball, with the centres running slowly outside him: it's then easier for the fullback to hit the line with a change of pace, and there's a greater margin of time for the stand-off or centre to hold the ball before passing;

2. get the man who is to give him the ball to run across (for example, the inside-centre in a dummy-switch with outside-centre, or the stand-off dummying to one or both of the centres) so that once again it's easy for the fullback to hit the line hard;

3. use the basic scrum to scrum-half timing device, with the scrum-half signalling to the fullback to start his run as soon as the ball is available, and calling for it and passing it at the point in the fullback's run established as right in practices.

And what about his line of run?
That's a matter of choice for him: he's running for space if he's the striker, and as straight as that will allow. In practice this means that he should be going across and straightening to run into the hole, rather than running on a simple diagonal (and that's not bad advice for all players covering in support). But he should stay aware of what he's asking of the other players involved. There's a limit as to how long any player can hold the ball before the opposition pressure gets to him.

What should the passer be looking for?
He's got to be looking for the fullback's appearance, of course, but he must also be looking for the space the fullback's running into. If it's being covered by the outside-centre drifting out, or the winger coming in, there's no point in holding the ball for the fullback: he doesn't want it.

It's highly desirable, too, that all the backs talk to each other, so that information is passed on. For example, the fullback himself should be able to see a drift defence and let the stand-off know at once. We're looking for space all the time.

You're also putting a premium on running speed?
Yes. Running speed is important as it minimises the time the cover defence has to saturate the field. The slower we get to the gain-line, the easier it is for them. Similarly, the less we stretch the opposing defence by making each pass a little longer, the easier it is for the cover to arrive. So we want forward speed and a

comfortably long basic pass to cut the cover out. Miss passes are also excellent for this, especially close to the opposition line.

And doesn't the flat pass affect this too?
Yes. Every time you pass the ball back a yard, you give the cover a yard. You buy lack of pressure from their front three by making it easier for their cover. The ideal is to polish the passing skills to the point where you can endure the pressure without too many problems, and cut out the cover by flat passing, long-passing, and high speed.

But doesn't the flat pass bring you under too much pressure?
Not if the stand-off is maintaining positional discipline, and creating the necessary space. But, of course, the flat pass is shorthand for pass as flat as you conveniently can. In the match you don't simply sling out flat passes if the player outside you isn't there to collect them. The flat pass is a device for concentrating support players' minds on where they should aim to be.

And is that true for all players, or just the backs?
It's true for everyone, though it may not always be possible. Getting into the right position may take a little longer, and even if we start as fast as we can, creating time by predicting exactly where we should turn up, it may not be on. And the same is true of our line of running. We have to make compromises because of lack of time (and sometimes that's down to fatigue), and the thing that suffers most is that compromise tends to be angle of run.

Going back to the backs, is there anything to be said about the position of the wingers?
A lot of their positioning should be covered in situation preparation. Far too often, wingers seem to have no clear idea of what their function is, and that's precisely the kind of detail to be sorted out in situation practices. But in general, it pays the winger to run off the player from whom he's going to get the ball. In other words, if you expect to receive from the fullback, make sure you're lining up off him rather than the centres. In general, most open-sided wingers in attack don't lie wide enough to be able always to run straight, or deep enough to hit the ball at pace. And, in general, they're very slow back into position if there's a check – a tackle, for example – just inside them: they over-run, and must fight to get back fast.

What happens when you start doing switches?
You've got to distinguish between the switch set up to gain a particular advantage and the switch employed to get out of difficulty. They're not different in kind – both employ the same techniques – but they're often different in the time available.

In the first kind, you start off with the final purpose: where do we want the striker to be running, and at what speed? His line of run is the most important element. Far too often when players do switches they can't actually choose their line of run – instead of ending up running straight into space, you find them being driven back into the opposition pack. There are times when you might employ a switch actually to do this – to get the ball back in front of your forwards – or have a player come in on that line as a dummy to check the opposing pack, but you want to do it by choice, and not because you can't control what you're doing.

Given that you've got the time – because of an early call, for example – you can easily arrange to have your striker choose whatever line of run he wishes, and, at the same time, whatever speed he wishes.

You're more limited when you're being forced into a switch, since you can't control your starting positions in the same way, and so it's more difficult to arrange the exact line of run of your striker. Still, against that you've a little better chance of the original ball-carrier being able to open up space. As he moves across bringing his opponent with him, he's opening up the space behind him into which the striker can run. You don't always get this effect in first phase, if your opponents are playing a zone defence against switches.

So how do you arrange the first-phase switch?
The only way to guarantee both direction and speed is to build it into your initial positioning.

You'll see that if you look at Fig. 19. Obviously, the only way that the inside-centre can end up running straight is if the stand-off brings the ball across the front of him. But you'll see that this cuts down on the inside-centre's acceleration – in fact, he may have to stand still for a moment. So he gets the ball on the right line but not running fast, and he's already wasted time – both of which points make it easier for the opposing cover to get to him.

This wouldn't matter if both players could go forward and pick up speed together, but then the odds are the inside-centre would have to check to let the stand-off get across. And besides, you don't have that much room with the opposing defence closing down on you.

Both of these problems disappear if you set it up initially. The simplest way of getting the striker running straight and fast is to position them as at opposite corners of a square, so that once they commit to the switch, they have equal distances to run (see Fig. 19).

How big a square?
The smaller it is, the longer they can delay committing themselves to the switch, and the less time the opposition have to react: but you pay for that advantage in terms of not clearing space, and perhaps getting two defenders very close to you. In attack, it always pays to think of space, getting enough room to work in, and so it's sensible to stay about the usual passing distance apart. If you get much wider than that, you have to start your switch very early, and this gives the opposition time to adjust.

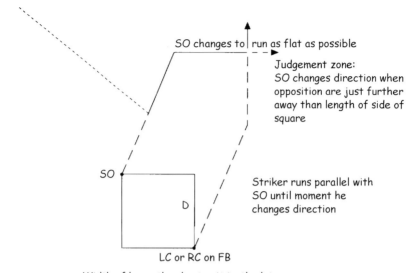

SO changes to run as flat as possible

Judgement zone:
SO changes direction when
opposition are just further
away than length of side of
square

SO

D

Striker runs parallel with
SO until moment he
changes direction

LC or RC on FB

Width of base: the shorter it is, the later you can
change direction. Maximum: distance between SO
and opposition at moment he receives the ball

Fig 19 Setting up switches in the first phase: the magic square
The diagram is set up to show how to get the striker running straight and fast –
but it will show you how to set up any desired line of strike. Just rotate the
square round SO until side D is pointing in the required direction. The striker
(LC, RC, FB) will then be in the right position relative to SO. Carry on as
before: the striker runs parallel with SO until there is a change of direction; he
then runs for a 90 degree intersection.

How about the timing of a switch?
Timing is just as important in a switch as, say, in a 2 v 1. If you pass too early in
a 2 v 1, the defender can take out the receiver; if you leave it too late, he can take
out the ball-carrier. In the middle there's the right time to pass – before the ball-
carrier is under pressure, but after the receiver is safe. That set-up remains true
whatever we do. If we complete our switch too early, the defender will take out the
receiver; if we leave it too late, we'll come under pressure, and the ball-carrier may
be taken out. So we have to judge when we do our switch.

How do we arrange that?
In just the same way. Our two players go forward, keeping the same relative
formation, to the point that's right. Just as with the 2 v 1, you learn that right point
by practising the switch against opposition. The aim is to control the timing, so
that whether they're rushing up to pressure you or hanging back in the hope that
you'll commit too early, you're judging when to start it.

And that's true of all switches?
I think so. If you take the switch between stand-off and outside centre you'll see it quite clearly. They'll be at opposite points of a big square; and, provided they stay that way, once they commit to the switch the outside-centre will always be running straight and fast.

The right moment comes in one of two ways. The obvious one is when they both go forward with the centre running parallel to the ball-carrier, to the point the ball-carrier feels is right, where upon he swings flat across field and the striker swings straight upfield. Less obvious is when they both start running flat across field – still, of course, staying in the relative positions – and when the receiver sees a suitable hole he swings straight into it. Of course, he has to be aware of how fast the opposition are coming up!

Doesn't the initial change of position give away what you're doing?
It gives away that you may be trying a switch . . . or a dummy-switch. You shouldn't know yourself which you're going to do until the latest possible moment. Ideally, you always get the opponent to commit himself before you do: that's precisely what you do in the 2 v 1, for example. So yes, you give something away, but the results justify it.

You mentioned that the opposition might hang back . . .
Yes. In fact, if the opposition are keeping you guessing with a variety of starts, it sometimes pays not to pressurise them – which they may expect – but to hang back in the hope that they get their timing wrong. You give away a certain amount of space, and that means you may not be able to do it close to your line, but in midfield it's quite a good test of their judgement.

One example of that is the use of drift defence at a line-out. If the opposition are consistently spinning the ball wide, it's futile trying to pressurise – that simply helps them to outflank you. So you go across and let them do their thing in front of you where you can see exactly what they're doing.

And a very clear example is what happens at a pivot penalty. In the case of such a penalty, the whole set-up is based on the probability that the defence will try to pressurise. For example, the distance from the scrum-half to the pivot has to be less than 10m, or the defenders would catch the pivot man. But if it's a lot less than 10m, the defenders will see where the ball has gone before they need to commit themselves: they can select the right target. And the distances of the other runners to that pivot man are fixed in the same way. All the runners must have had their chance before the opposition cover the 10m (or whatever distance the attackers decide by taking the ball back behind the point). But if the defence doesn't pressurise, most of these fine adjustments are futile. The fixed pivot deprives the attackers of judgement – at least the first time they try it.

What happens if, in midfield, the defenders don't pressurise? They get a clear view of who's got the ball before they need to commit, and should have the advantage. Of course, that merely presents the intelligent coach with a future opportunity to develop the move.

Are there any other cases when the opposition might hang back?
There's one case when they have to hang back – behind their goal line when you're taking a tap penalty 5m out. They can't cross the goal-line till you've played the ball. This means that if the attacking team's timing is right, they can have all their forwards in full stride, taking the ball as flat as possible from a scrum-half who has worked out exactly how late he can afford to play the ball. And the defenders have to hang around and wait for them to arrive, then try to stop them inside the 5m (see Fig. 20).

Opposition goal line								
				9	•			
Our players	2	7	4		5	6	8	
		1				3		
Indicated by	1	2				3	4	fingers

Fig 20 Using space efficiently: a 5m penalty
9 stands to the left of the ball and looks at 3. 3 checks where the opposition defence is weak, and indicates by showing 1, 2, 3 or 4 fingers to 9. 9 then relays the strike point in the same way to all the other players. You work out start positions by trial and error; ensure that the depth of the receivers is adequate to allow them to take the ball running near top speed. He moves to the same side of the ball as the call, but remains a metre away. Then he claps his hand, and everyone runs straight forward. At a moment established in practice, he plays the ball and passes to the designated receiver. Never use the locks (4 and 5) unless there's a big hole in front of them.

But quite often they do.
Yes, but only when the attackers haven't used space properly. The attacking forwards need to be well spread out, stretching the defence, and the attack must be launched where the opposition defence is weak.

How do you do that?
Once the attacking forwards are in position, one of them signals to the scrum-half where the best strike point is. It's better that way, because the opposition will be keeping an eye on the scrum-half, and the forward can inspect the whole line of defenders in front of him without making it obvious. Then the scrum-half signals to all his forwards, so they know where the strike will be. Scrum-half signals for

the start, and they all gallop forward, with the ball being fed as late as possible to the designated receiver.

That's a bit like a pivot . . .
Yes. It's fixed in position. But this time the distance from that point to the score-line is so critical that it doesn't matter. You can see, though, how futile it would be to take the position back a couple of metres: that would be a gift to the opposition. And if the point was 10m out, it would be sheer good luck if the start worked at all.

That's the kind of thinking that lies behind preparing 'situations'?
Exactly. If you have a potent weapon it pays to reserve it for the occasion when it'll really work; and you don't want to squander possession trying it where it probably won't work. It also lets you get into operation fast and without fuss – especially if you've been playing 'thematic unopposed' with penalties as your theme.

Wouldn't it be equally futile to pass the ball back?
You mean in that tap penalty? Yes. It would be exactly the same as moving the point back that distance. And it's just the same wherever you pass the ball back. It always gives the opposition that little bit longer to adjust their defence. Whenever you can it pays to pass flat. Of course, at any particular moment in the match you won't be able to do it, because your supporters haven't managed to get into the right position; it always comes back to the control of support positioning. The more often they can get into position to run on to the flat pass in space, the more successful you'll be.

And in the backs, you're looking for the stand-off to create the space that lets the backs do this?
Yes. If he does, it lets us adopt a flatter line which offers every advantage possible over the tucked-in line.

Earlier on you talked about 'creating space'. What did you mean?
Every time you open up space to clear a channel for attack you're 'creating' it – well, it didn't exist before. I mentioned it once in terms of a switch, where the ball-carrier pulls a defender across with him, and lets the striker run into the resultant space. You get the same effect when a winger swings out, taking a defender with him, and passes back inside over his shoulder to a supporter running into that space.

Another implied creation of space was when we looked at that penalty near the line and how the attackers can create space by their own formation – forcing the opposing defence to leave wider gaps in trying to cover them. You can do precisely the same thing with your back division, and at the same time force the opposing cover to run that much further in each phase.

Again, when you're setting up a tap penalty or a short line-out, it pays to keep your forwards as a compact threat. The opposition forwards have to cover them, and that stops them spreading out. That way, you preserve space. That was one of the early advantages of the pivot penalty: it really held the opposition in, and preserved space for attack. Of course, what you're doing is simply copying the structure of the game, where having scrums, and mauls, and rucks, and line-outs is basically a way of clearing the pitch – creating space for attacks. However, to some extent that has been destroyed by importing the R.L. spread defence.

And are these the only ways of creating space?
No – we haven't considered several of the most basic and important ways of creating space.

Think of opening a channel for attack. If we can do that, and bring an extra man in as ball-carrier, we create the simplest, most effective form of attack.

We can do it very simply by establishing 'edges' to the channel, with the player who will give the pass running straight and the player on the further edge of the channel keeping wide. Or think of a scrum on the right near touch, with a back-row attack lined up: they want their winger to lie wide to open up that channel. If this opponent doesn't lie wide to cover him, there's a chance of switching the focus of attack to the winger.

We can create a channel for a very swift winger, by closing up our entire back-division so that the ball can reach him with one, or at most two passes, and leaving a deal of space outside him.   More radically, we can create space by our formation in the backs, especially from those tactical points where we're confident of getting the ball. The most obvious example of this is clearing the right side of the field for back-row attack. Most back-row attacks are limited in making ground – the players keep running into defenders. But at a centrefield scrum where we're odds on to get the ball, we can put our stand-off and centres on the left, and open up a very wide channel. Our winger would be out on touch. If we set it up quickly and smoothly we can get our second runner into a long channel. And that same wide channel can be exploited by attacks from the backs using the timing device I've already described. We can do the same to the left if we're being wheeled in the scrum. I'm sure this will be developed in the future.

Are there any ideas about space that apply particularly to the forwards?
I don't think so, but there are some which are very important to any group running as a group. Far and away the most important idea is that of creating width and depth, both in attack and defence. If you think of the locus of the ball as the axis of the group you'll see it clearly. We want a distribution of players on either side of that axis – to give choice in the distribution of the ball in attack, and to avoid being outflanked in defence. We also want depth – to make sure we don't over-run a check in attack, and to catch the elusive runner in defence.

You see the same principles very clearly in back-division defence, with the front three seeking to use width to trap the opposition, and the back three providing depth against the kicks that may result.

In attack especially, forwards don't think enough about creating width and depth. It's understandable: they're conditioned to think of contact with the opposition and setting up rucks and mauls as their function, and often this makes those rucks and mauls inevitable. But a pack that believes in its passing and creates space is extremely hard to stop.

There's one particular respect in which the forwards can create space, and that's by driving in the set-pieces, and forcing the opposing back row to stay down. This can be valuable, but the sides that do it often go on too long in a kind of laborious attack. Once the opposing pack has been pulled together, we would aim to get the ball fast into the resultant space, by feeding forwards lying off, for example, or letting the scrum-half run with support.

At this point in 1993 we broke off. But here we are again, older if not wiser.

You'd been talking about making space for more effective forward attack. You must have been pleased to watch the All Blacks in the first World Cup.
Of course. 'Total rugby' was the buzz phrase and the development of forwards into more complete footballers one of the first fruits. And it's even beginning to happen here. At the start of the '99 Calcutta Cup the England forwards launched an admirable series of attacks. They made space and used it in three ways:

1. ball-carriers had space to beat a man – space to check, dummy, roll-off tackles, side-step, swerve, change direction, hand off: they set out to stay on their feet, and keep the ball in their hands ready to pass. When the tackle seemed inevitable, they turned their back on the tackler and fed a supporter behind them;

2. supporters worked to maintain useful space – space to accelerate into, space to carry the ball forward into, and depth to provide for cover. They too focused on staying on their feet, going forward and being ready to transfer the ball; and

3. it was a genuine group activity, with everyone concentrated on furthering the group purpose – to maintain a dynamic attack.

All of this denied the Scots what they dearly wanted – a simple target, a single focus for aggressive defence. Even when a player went to ground, the ball was recycled fast and space maintained. For several minutes it looked as though England would run up a cricket score. There seemed to be no answer to such a varied, dynamic attack.

But that space had to be created . . .
Created, maintained and recreated. As soon as the pack stopped focusing on that, they began to converge, and rucks and mauls became almost inevitable.

And that's what happened?
Yes, happily for Scotland the England forwards reverted to habit. Each ball-carrier,

for whatever reason (though I suspect the onset of fatigue) began running into defenders and going to ground. Immediately, the momentum of attack diminished and everything slowed down. What had been dynamic became semi-static. And something glorious, exciting, entertaining and effective disappeared from the match – to my relief as a Scot, but my regret as the proponent of total rugby. What was tactically interesting was that it never reappeared. If it was impossible to maintain continuously, attempts might have been made to resurrect it in critical situations – for example the opposing 22 – or times – for example the start and end of each half. However, it seems that it has appeared again in the Welsh match this year so there's hope it may take root.

Incidentally, another point needs to be made: the forwards who took part in the open attack were the big forwards who later did such powerful rucking. 'Big' doesn't necessarily imply thick, clumsy, or one-directional. That's usually what bad coaching (not just by coaches) tends to propagate, but it ain't necessarily so.

Some players thrive on such an image. Conversion won't be easy.
Who mentioned 'easy'? But you've the international example, and the ambition of the younger players to have a brighter future and a more satisfying present. They can provide leverage on those happy in their stereotype of hard, if limited, players. You could show *them* clips of Keith Wood in action. But technically it's not that difficult: I remember working on swerving with a No. 8 who played for Swansea and was on the edge of the England squad. A few minutes later in a practice match he produced a beauty to beat the England fullback. You'll find all the technical stuff covered in *Total Rugby*.

As I've mentioned once or twice, everyone was very elusive in the school playground: it just needs to be reactivated. Then they can incorporate their skills in intensive small-sided touch rugby. Make clear that you expect everyone to be taking part, at every practice, before you appear, and then do some swift coaching on what you observe. You'll find a crib sheet in *Total Rugby* (pp. 136–9) as well. When you incorporate this in unit practice, bring out the need to launch the attack from situations in which you've got their pack on the back foot so that your forwards can join in fast. Start from a drive at a line-out, where it's comparatively easy to shift them and still have one or two spare men on the fringes. Hammer home immediately the need to be ready to beat defenders and transfer the ball fast.

Fine! Here you are an OAP (a senior citizen!) and still sparking with enthusiasm.
Ah, in my imagination I'm watching a Loughborough pack of lads scoring from just such a space attack against Gloucester 30 years ago. I've recently learned to listen to my body – one long complaint – so I'm mining my experience. Mind you, without the imagination to devise and improve practices, solve problems, and sort out new approaches, a coach is crippled in what should be his constant aim – to improve. You set out for an unattainable ideal, which is why you can never be

satisfied with your present attainment. And that's an attitude you try to transfer to your best players.

And adopting open attack is part of that process in your forwards?
Of course. They deserve the opportunity to maximise their potential. I hope they're well on their way. They want to be complete footballers with specific positional strengths in a team of footballers with specific positional strengths. As coach, you should be holding that ideal before them. Not everyone develops it for himself. We need to disabuse them of imaginary constraints.

So you'd like to see the end of serial rucking?
Not at all. For a given team, at a given point, in a given match, it may be a necessity. It's the kind of accustomed activity that can settle a team down, restore confidence, slow the game to a pace at which they're happy, wear down a lighter opposition, deprive the opposition backs of the ball, get the team back into focus.

But it certainly needs monitoring. It has a hypnotic rhythm and can soon become mechanical, with players willing to plunge forward for minimal gain without thought of alternatives. It resembles the deadly impact of the five-tackle rule on some league forwards: whatever happens, you mustn't lose possession, and you do that by hanging on like grim death till you're tackled and relieved of responsibility. And the fifth receiver whacks it down the field to the waiting back three who may or may not be more enterprising. Now that's not inevitable: have you seen the Australian League XIII? It's magic (ask the England XIII) with supremely fit, fast, skilful, confident athletes who look on every possession as a chance to score a try. It's an ideal model for what we might dream of our forwards doing in open attack. Of course, our forwards can continue their attack only by working round a central axis (the principle behind the valuable 1–5 exercise in *Total Rugby*, which a TV clip showed the England forwards working on).

No. What I'm saying is that serial rucking is OK if it's dynamic, carrying a real threat of a decisive breakaway, sucking in defenders. To achieve this you need to do what we've already discussed. The aim of the ball-carrier is not to run into an opponent and slump to the ground. It's to make intending tacklers miss you, so you can carry the ball that much further forward. And if you can't avoid the obstacle, drive up into him and keep your legs working as if you were running uphill. You've got to focus on going forward not going down. If the first two or three players can do this, it gets easier for the rest – space opens up.

But if you ruck passively, semi-statically, it can be dangerous.

Dangerous? To the players?
No, well not necessarily, but dangerous tactically, and perhaps to the game itself. If your rucking is slow, mechanical, predictable, it allows the opponents to detach two or three forwards to join the back defence. This deprives your backs of space to attack by handling, and they may feel they have to kick – to the waiting back

three. Does that sound familiar? With the added players the defence can string across the field as in league. The laws of rugby union were devised to create situations in which a large number of players are confined to a limited area, leaving space for handling attacks. Inefficient rucking and mauling erode that margin. Add in aggressive, pressurising, head-on tackling, as well as drift defence – all of which I've encouraged enthusiastically – and handling attack becomes increasingly difficult. One measure is that Australia conceded only one try in winning the 1999 World Rugby Cup while England lost to South Africa by five drop goals. Defence, in fact, has always been easier to organise and implement than attack, and attack has developed by finding appropriate answers. This underlines the importance of developing all forms of dynamic forward attack, and the key to that is a determination to go forward supported by radically improved evasive and handling skills. Dynamic forward attacks create the ideal launch-pad for handling attacks by the backs – though of course they lead to frequent scores in their own right.

Can the backs do much to advance their own cause?
I'm sure they can, but before we get to them we must make a critical point. Even a dynamic forward attack creates only a momentary advantage during which the opposing defence is disorganised. It's vital that that moment should not be lost in indecision by the forwards or the backs. The ball must come back immediately the scrum-half demands it, and the backs must know precisely how they can best use it. We need high-level discipline to make the most of the moment. As soon as the forwards are substantially checked, they're expecting the call. And all the way up the pitch behind the forwards, the halves must be actively considering their options. At moments like this, preparedness is all. It may be that one of the halves thinks that a break is on for himself; it may be an overload on the right or a deserted blind-side on the left. But the great thing is to be ready for it and go for it.

But not a time for kicking . . .
Well, never say never – seconds to go, a point behind, just outside the 22, an excellent drop kicker . . . but of course you're right: it would have to be a special case.

You said you were sure that the backs could do something to help themselves. What did you have in mind?
Many three-quarter lines deny themselves breathing space: they put themselves under unnecessarily heavy pressure in what often looks like a fashion take on a flawed dogma: 'Thy starting position shall be as near to the gain-line as possible.' In the first edition of *Total Rugby* I tried to point out how wasteful and potentially dangerous a deep line was. I suggested a shallow wide line was a far better attacking platform. That remains, I think, true. But at the very least you need an acceleration zone, a choice of running line, and ideally a chance to set your opponent up. You need – and are entitled to – a certain amount of depth. Without that, you're almost certain to lose the initiative – not only your personal initiative,

in other words the power to do what you'd like or what you'd intended, but also the team initiative, or what they have worked for. At best, you may find yourself forced inside towards the opposition pack; at worst, you offer yourself up for opposition tackling practice. It's always been tough in the centre, but with no space it's ridiculous. Even with space, it's all too easy to waste it by shuffling forward before you know the fly-half has the ball. That's something you certainly can't afford to do, because unhappily the opposition can start moving as soon as the ball emerges. In a pressurised situation like this whatever you do tends to be flurried and inaccurate. You may even try to play rugby going backwards, making a bad situation rapidly worse.

The most extreme form of this is found when fly-halves take up, as a matter of course, fashionably flat positions regardless of the situation. If your forwards are playing a dynamic game and providing excellent ball, that positioning works. However, if your forwards are under pressure and the opposing backs are in the set position, it doesn't. Not for you and certainly not for your centres. You immediately lose the initiative because you have no time to do anything well. You must either adapt your positioning to the balance of the pack, or make sure your scrum-half deals with all the ball. Do what's best for the team, whether it's fashionable or not.

You don't go much on fashion, but you're in favour of new ideas . . .
They're two very different things. People adopt fashions to create an impression; people examine new ideas to see what's to be gained and under what conditions. Fashions tend to adopt what's easiest to copy. Standing with your feet apart isn't going to turn you into a world-class place kicker. You have to sort out the essential from the superficial and be quite clear about limitations that apply. It's usually a gradual learning process. The positioning of the fly-half is simply a case in point.

But you still cling to the notion of the running fly-half.
Yes, for the reasons given in this book. It's so old an idea now that it deserves to be treated as a new one! I bet the centres will benefit in terms of space and acceleration. Failing that, they'd certainly benefit from applying the suggestions in *Total Rugby* (pp.256–7) for establishing their start positions. To modify them for a standing fly-half, all you need is to think of the inside-centre as if he were fly-half, with the standing fly-half as his scrum-half.

But doesn't that highlight the delay imposed on the centres and the advantage given to the defenders?
I think so. It certainly deserves a bit of thought and investigation.

Part of the continuing education of the coach and the player?
You may smile, but if coaches and players gave themselves time to cultivate a critical habit of mind, they'd be better at their job and far more involved personally in their work. They could test a new idea and put fashion to flight!

Don't you think you expect too much of the coach?
Your average coach has never had more reason to be ambitious; your average paid player has never had more reason to work towards becoming a top-grade coach. I've taken coaching seriously because I feel I owe it to the players – just as I have worked for all my students. And it's been great: I recommend it!

Do you think coaching has improved?
Oh yes, but look at the number of imported coaches (and imported players) in all our games. We seem to specialise in producing absentee coaches. Like the absentee landlords in 19th-century north-west Scotland, they have the title and they take the money, but they don't get involved, and they don't do any good. Watch TV clips of soccer sides training, and all too often you'll see a figure in the background, swathed against the cold but not even watching the players at work. They mistake what I've called 'coaching situations' for coaching. They don't get in there, creating enthusiasm and eliminating the cause of mistakes. They depend on the players to improve by a process akin to osmosis. It was summed up for me by an FA First Division manager. He'd ordered half a dozen copies of *Total Rugby* so I rang him up.

'Do you do much coaching?' I asked him.

'No,' he said. 'I buy the players because they can play.'

Now, I've never met a player that couldn't be improved in some aspect of his play, and the very best players are those keenest to learn. And in a sense it's with them that a coach's work is most valuable and most interesting. Talent is a valuable asset that must be helped to develop. I remember an attempt to set me up in New Zealand, when they gave me a potential All Black scrum-half to coach. He could pass a phenomenal distance – which was bound, I reckoned, to mean a certain amount of inaccuracy. So I spent a very happy hour with him establishing models for his passes, and was lucky enough to produce really consistent results. He was delighted, I was very happy, and the organiser was amazed. He said it had never crossed his mind that such an obviously talented player needed coaching. The lad did become an All Black, and the organiser became one of my best friends. And in a professional setting, you've really got to maximise the value of your investment.

That's why I'd like our top rugby coaches to emulate the top golf coaches – the coaches who work with the top pros to iron out their difficulties. To do that the coach must never tire of demanding technical excellence. But before he can do that he's got to be able to pinpoint what is going wrong, and specify how to put it right. You can do it only on an individual basis, but it's easy to organise time for it, before, during or after the squad session. It's the most satisfying aspect of technical coaching.

We have a National Coaching Foundation which is producing a great deal of relevant material, but the individual sport, the individual club, the individual coach, have to show willing to benefit from it.

Technical coaching is only part of the job: it equips the individual, the unit, the team, with a repertoire of abilities, established by intensive practice and related to the situations that arise in the game. And if the work is accompanied by a genuinely positive attitude in the coach – enthusiastic, appreciative and supportive – it starts to foster similar values in the players. This is an extremely important step in getting players moving on the road to taking responsibility for demanding high standards of themselves. We want them to supply the energy and commitment to self-improvement. When they start coming to you with, 'I'm not happy with my passing off my left hand', you feel happy, and when they start offering sensible analyses and hypotheses, you're laughing. I've no means of knowing how common this now is, but it's important because players like that will become the coaches of the future.

To judge from the standard of performance at international level, there has been a substantial improvement in the range and quality of skills on display. But there's still room to improve the quality and especially the consistency of performance. You see some lamentable efforts with individual skills. And as I've been saying, I think we get ourselves into unit trouble by failing to recognise the tactical limitations of what's fashionable at the moment. I sometimes wonder if the back three have been given adequately clear criteria for launching counter-attacks. But there's no doubt that the trend is upward, and for that we should be grateful.

It's more difficult to judge the inspirational input of coaches. Ideally (to my way of thinking) they'd embody confident, constructive leadership devoid of cycnicism and institutional intimidation. Even in professional rugby, despite Lombardi, there are things more important than winning. That's probably as good a note to start 2000 on as any.

ADVANTAGE RUGBY – CONSISTENT CREATION OF SPACE

What we're moving towards in terms of team tactics is an overall game plan based on a strategy – the basic staple use you'll make of the ball – and tactics to meet recurrent situations.

In planning these tactics you may look for a simplifying principle, a single aim that will give your tactics coherence as well as variety, and which may help simplify the thinking of the TDM. The simplest and most effective one I know is 'advantage rugby'. It's based on the consideration that whenever we have problems in getting more than our share of the ball, we must arrange to use it to maximum advantage. To do that we want always to have the odds in our favour. There are various ways we might do that, but the simplest in concept and implementation, and the most clear cut in effect, is always to arrange a numerical advantage. We don't play 3 v 3 or 4 v 4 because it doesn't give us an edge: we're looking always to have one more player available than they have. The extra man is the situation we're always trying to create by all the more or less complicated means at our disposal, so it pays to consider the simple arrangements made possible by an understanding of space and timing:

- we identify space easy to attack with an extra man or we create space easy to attack with an extra man;
- we identify the players who can function as an extra man (stand-off switching sides, fullback, winger on non-attacking side, forward or scrum-half in back-row attacks, spare forward among the backs);
- we concentrate technical attention on perfecting the simple skills needed to make it work.

The overall aim in all we do now is to have our striker running into space, with less need to try difficult skills, and less chance of the attack being checked and our losing possession.

This may not be achieved 100% even by the most expert use of our resources, but if we can edge up the percentage of times we achieve it, our scoring rate will go up quite dramatically.

Furthermore, this is an example of team planning and organisation reducing the demands upon our players. We can't always have very gifted players available to us, but we can use the players we do have more effectively.

The implication for the coach is that in every situation his first thought will be for the simple way of creating the numerical advantage. He looks for the space, selects the extra man, uses space/timing technique to get him into operation, plays it and refines it in practice. For the TDM, too, it is a matter of asking first: 'Where can we most easily get the extra man?' And he will be guided by the preliminary work done by the coach.

Once you've designed a few of these gambits, you can start building them into practices. It's easy to see how they would get into unit sequences, and playing the sequence reveals the way in which the regular extra man can function effectively. You can't expect a fullback, for example, to come in as extra man in first phase and again on the resultant blind-side – far better to have the stand-off switching into the blind. And it's the same for all the exercises suggested in Part Three – it's simply a matter of fitting in the theme of the extra man. This might culminate in a version of thematic unopposed in which from every tactical point you are introducing the spare player.

I should reaffirm that 100% is very improbable, though during two seasons in Japan, with a lot of time and very willing players, we must have been achieving the extra man in a very substantially improved ratio over normal play.

Second, there's no reason to suppose that the players named above are the only ones who can provide the extra man. But they are the obvious ones. The wings and fullback are effective because their opponents cannot simply commit themselves to the running threat: they are also the depth defence. The stand-off is effective because he can use the forward mass at the tactical point to let him elude his immediate opponent, and at some of these points (for example, mauls and rucks) he won't even be faced by back row forwards. Centres, on the other hand, are faced by immediate opponents with a single aim; they can be used but it inevitably means a certain amount of complexity.

Third, the method will function more easily and effectively once you have established basic tempo control, and are playing at a pace dictated by yourselves. This means hard work with the forwards on getting the ball to the back of every scrum, maul, ruck as fast as possible, and holding it there ready to give the scrum-half when he wants it, and the scrum-half monitoring the time needed to impose the extra-man pattern at each point.

But perhaps the key need is high fitness and discipline in the backs, and particularly in the strikers. They are going to benefit most from this scheme in terms of attacking opportunities, and they must give a lot to it. Discipline means above all getting fast into position, even when they are tired. This is going to be the critical factor in determining the tempo that the team can use. It also means remaining alert to defensive team duties. If two of the back three, that little defensive team responsible for deep defence, are functioning in attack, the third must make sure that the ground is covered against counter-attack.

It's fair to point out, however, that though additional stress is placed on our back three, it does involve some of our most talented runners far more thoroughly in our game, and the consistent pattern of extra men does impose a load on the opposition. Typically this kind of rugby – like the better-known overlap rugby – has the effect of forcing the opposition cover to run far and fast. It evidently leads to many wide breaks, and against a handling attack (as opposed to a kicking attack, where often the ball is obviously going to touch or to a deep defender) the cover has a constant sense of the need to get there fast. This will bring pressure to bear on the opposition pack, especially if their forte is power rather than mobility.

A more radical development occurred to me in Japan in 1980 – using twin fullbacks in attack. This was prompted by two things: we'd two very good attacking fullbacks; and at Loughborough we'd already looked at using two lines in attack in sevens. In the sevens, I thought in terms of a four-man front line, with our three best runners lying back. This gave us a chance of strikers coming from deep, running on interesting angles, and calling for the ball when there was space. (It also meant that if one of the front four came under pressure, he could roll it back, confident that it would be snapped up by one of the second line.) The same possibilities seemed to be available in the full game. We didn't persevere with it because there was already a danger of mental and emotional indigestion in the players, but it bears looking at again.

Part Five

Building an enterprising repertoire

Phil Greening in the first Six Nations Competition

Phil Greening demonstrates that you can be big without being thick. Here he observes the first rule of dynamic forward attack – he's running into space and intent on going forward. He has already come some distance and evaded the temptation early on to do the 'safe' thing and go to ground. But the second rule is to check out your support – it takes no more than a moment to look about you – and get into shape to give him the ball. Tucking the ball into your armpit is not a recommended gambit. The supporter to his left has problems – for instance, the French leg over which he's about to trip – but it's unlikely that he has responded soon enough to the developing situation. He's being occluded by the French forward, and hasn't registered that Greening may well be checked and need close support. It's not good enough to be thereabouts in support – you've got to be *there*.

9 **Developing fresh ideas**

CREATING AN ENTERPRISING ATTACK

We can't divorce enterprise from efficiency. We have two basic needs, far more important than enterprise as such:

1. quality performance – it's better to concentrate on a few highly polished, completely trusted starts, than any number of inadequately prepared, ill-understood 'novelties';
2. speed of selection – a wide choice is a slow choice: at any particular point, our TDM wants to be selecting from a limited range of options.

Without these qualities, enterprise is simply pie in the sky.

However, if we want to turn a high proportion of possession into points, we need to be more than efficient – we need to be enterprising. And we need to find enterprising answers to three kinds of question.

1. **Our strategy**
- How do we clear the channel?
- How can we vary the way we get the ball into it?
- How can we vary the striker(s)?

2. **The results of our strategy**
- How do we exploit the kind of space we'll be left with if our basic strike is checked?
- How do we exploit the compromises our basic pattern imposes on their defence?

3. **Our tactics**
- How do we exploit the major recurrent situations?

Where do we find enterprising answers?

1. In our brains – and the following few pages are devoted to a few hints, tips, and examples.

2. In books – and the pages after that are devoted to a whole series of starts that have stood the test of time and competition. There's nothing there that's mere theory.

3. Increasingly from watching rugby on television. There's no doubt that even at the top level – where they're often inhibited by fear of failure rather than inspired by opportunity – teams are playing more enterprising, better prepared rugby. Don't watch to be entertained: watch to learn!

You know the channel in which you are best able to strike. Go through this section and select ways of getting the ball there, and variations once you've got it there. The diagrams are precise: look at them carefully, and study them till you can feel them in your heart. Pick the simplest under each heading, and work out how you'd introduce it. Be ready to apply the model, your expectations of problems, and so on. Of course, it won't be easy.

Look at the space you'll have left. Search through again for a way to exploit that. This is your first sequence – and it may well be your first original rhythm (see page 82 ff.).

What do you think the opposition will do to stop your basic pattern? What can you do to exploit the weakness they've left elsewhere? Look through again.

Now pick just one situation which you know you'll face and from which you ought to be able to score. Think of your players. Go through again and pick a start that will utilise what they've got to offer.

Now think of your opponents: will that come as a surprise to them?

This is a fairly straightforward, down-to-earth process. Every example offered represents a practical answer to a problem. These ideas work if the coach really understands them, and presents them properly. Explain them, walk through them, trot through them, fine-tune them – one at a time. Better one really solid than three soft-centred.

TRYING SOMETHING NEW

Everyone can devise something new in rugby coaching. As coaching develops this becomes a little more difficult, but it still remains a realistic aim.

You've got to give yourself a chance, though. You've got to tune in to your perceptions and, as soon as you get a signal, stop and take it seriously. It's very much the same pattern of investigation as that suggested in Chapter 1, but it's working not so much on what happens out there as on the interest it generates in your head. If something strikes you as an interesting possibility, look at it, and let your imagination play around with it. The 'something' might be a fluke occurrence, something you've never seen before. Equally, it might be an answer to a particular problem that you face this particular season in your club. Or it might be a development so natural that several coaches pick it up individually at about the same time.

Here are some examples working up to the production of a new unit start:

Intensive handling

Starting every session with intensive, quality-controlled, small-group handling is a great investment: it pays off every time. But it's also a great area in which to experiment. You can devise new variations on old ideas:

- make the players aware of space. Start off continuous looping across the pitch from the 22; the natural movement will take them to the goal-line – but they mustn't cross it – there's got to be a call for a change of direction . . . and again as they approach the 22 again;
- make them change the focus of attack. At a call they break from one exercise – looping, say – to another, for example spinning the ball wide;
- give them a programme. With five in a line, you can have them set up very complicated patterns that they enjoy and that demand control of space (see Fig. 21);
- give them more active opposition. Put a defender on each line across the pitch. He's allowed to move forward from the line 10m or so against any particular opponent, but no more than that. Run your handling exercises against them;

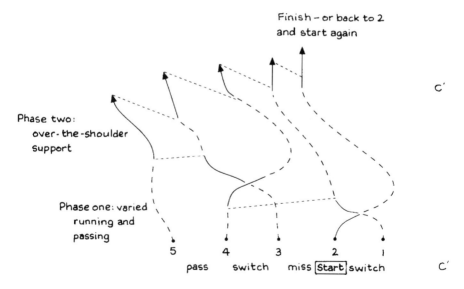

Fig. 21 A variety show

- time their runs, measure their passes. Give each group a set task and measure their speed. If you don't have a watch, use other measures; for example, how many speed passes can you make trotting between touch and the near post?

It's also a fertile ground for developing new skills, so that our players can keep the ball alive in a greater variety of circumstances. Consider this example:

Topic: passing the ball over the shoulder when the player is being forced across (for example a winger).

First recognition: at Middlesex Sevens: a forward about to be buried by A. McHarg passes back over his shoulder. Our centre scores. We go on to win the tournament.

Idea: why shouldn't all our players learn to do that efficiently?

Procedure:

- establish a clear model of the pass, i.e. get the ball high, establish normal reception area, apply basic model of passing;
- get them used to it in small groups;
- devise intensive handling exercises:
  (i) group of five runs in line down 5m line, leader with ball. He swerves out towards touch, and passes the ball back to 2 on the line, and joins the back of the line. 2 repeats. When not actually passing, everyone stays on the line;
  (ii) same exercise down 5m line, but players choose whether to swerve left or right of the line. The swerve is designed to take a defender out, leaving space for the next man – swerve with commitment;
  (iii) same exercise but this time with opposition. As soon as 1 has passed to 2, he sets off to catch him. 2 then has to reach 3 over 1's head. As soon as he's done this, 2 tries to catch 3, while 1 gets back on the line. (This was devised by a RN syndicate on the Summer School Advanced Course.);
- incorporate it in handling by backs and unopposed: for example, the ball must always come back across the line once it reaches the wing: each player supports, still running out, and the ball comes back again and again over the inside shoulder;
- run it against the defensive system outlined in (ii) above.

Or this one:

Topic: spin passing for everyone.

First recognition: we'd think it odd if our scrum-half didn't spin pass off the ground or in dive pass: the ball goes further, faster, more accurately.

Idea: we'll extend it to all our backs (then all our players).

Procedure:

- establish a clear model of the pass – it's mechanically identical to spin punting, and should be introduced in precisely the same way:
  (i) long axis of ball at right angles to long axis of hand;
  (ii) spin starts by ball rolling down fingers – face your partner, step forward and roll it to him like bowls at knee level – don't turn your hand over;
  (iii) turn at right angles and repeat to the partner across the body, gradually turning the ball to point towards him;
- replace all 'normal' passes in intensive handling with spin-passing. (This initially spread in France and Wales and is now orthodox.)

Personal skills

Of course, it needn't be restricted to passing. Every one of our present ortho-doxies started off as some player's or coach's heresy. And often enough the problem lies less in devising an effective new form than in getting fashion-conscious players to adopt it.

Topic: reversed foot jumping at 2 in the line-out.

First Recognition: an opponent in a UAU match at Loughborough who consistently took his own ball despite being small. (He may have picked it up from the Japanese, but I certainly hadn't seen it before he used it.)

Idea: big jumpers using that method will be dominant – it gives a long, flat, fast take-off stride, from near the midline in front of the opponent. It's ideal for a timed throw. It offers excellent disguise.

Procedure:

- establish a clear model of the jump;
- get front jumpers doing it to slap basketball backboard – establish its merits;
- get timed throw organised;
- explain changes in blocking – front blocker going across at right angles; rear blocker working hard to keep him high;
- feed the hooker!

Devising new starts for backs

This brings us to our real concern – how we create greater variety in our back play. We need variations that will allow us to disguise our strategy so that we maintain some surprise though continuing to strike in our staple channel; we need starts that will allow us to exploit situations.

These starts combine what we've done in space and time, and what we've done on judgement: they won't work well if inadequately understood, inadequately practised, or applied with inadequate judgement.

What follows is a worked example – a real case of how such a start comes into being. You'll see that it's not at all glossy in the early stages, no matter how polished it may appear in the match.

As often happens, it started with a problem: our centres could make little contribution in attack. We had a potentially excellent young stand-off; a fullback who was to play for All Japan under-23s, very quick, elusive, and attack-minded; and an excellent, outstandingly quick left wing who'd all but given up the game because of recurrent shoulder injuries. In other words, we had a potentially powerful strike force if we could launch fullback and wing into space.

The first task, long before we reached putting them together, was to convince the wing that he could play: getting him hyper-fit and showing him how to fall. He became a match winner, and toured New Zealand with the All Japan under-23s (and the fullback).

I'd already got everyone spin passing. It was there the idea was born of a double miss in which the ball went direct from stand-off to fullback across the front of both centres. This was a case of an idea emerging in the fullness of time: when I got back to the UK I found that Bristol and France were both using a simpler version. They introduced the fullback directly as a third centre: I'd set out to make his entry itself part of the surprise.

Out of a kind of academic interest I'd got the stand-off practising very long passes – set him up with a 'centre' on either side of him, and gradually moved them further and further out. He was almost equally good off either hand (but when it came to matches we restricted it to movements to the left). His long pass looked just as sound as his normal pass.

At that point I got our fullbacks – I'd been working on the idea of fielding twin fullbacks – and got them running on to this long pass. It was absolutely straightforward to establish how far ahead of the fullback the ball should be passed to let him run fast on to it, and there was no problem in taking the spinning ball – stand-offs do it all the time, and we were doing it all the time in intensive handling.

As soon as the idea emerged, I started drawing little diagrams – like the diagrams in this book. By assuming all the players are running at the same speed, you can work out the kind of compromises that make it work. You start altering start positions, lines of run, times of start, and if need be speed – you're seeking as ever to find ways of having one player arrive at a certain point, running on a certain line, at a certain speed. The complication this time was how we were going to get an effective compromise between the running of the fullback and the running of the centres.

In all planning, it pays to start with the *final purpose*. We had the fullback running into space wide of the centres, but to give him that space we had to make sure their outside centre didn't drift out. We had, therefore, to exercise *judgement* in the timing of his run and the timing of the pass to him. If he emerged too early he'd attract attention, and if the pass were made too early he'd become a target. Ideally, he'd emerge and the ball would reach him when the opponents were almost on top of the centres – committed to their own men. I drew Fig. 22, and thought about it.

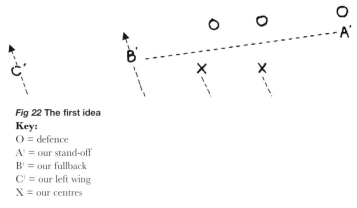

Fig 22 The first idea
Key:
O = defence
A¹ = our stand-off
B¹ = our fullback
C¹ = our left wing
X = our centres

Thinking isn't something you can organise overmuch. The best ideas usually come when you're relaxed and easy: Archimedes was undoubtedly in a bath of pleasantly hot water when the significance of the splashing hit him. Ideas start with a numb feeling, and diagrams are simply ways of escaping from it.

It was evident, though, that the stand-off was going to have to judge the timing of his long pass, and that meant he had to be able to carry the ball. I already knew two ways he could do this: by running on to it slowly, and by running across – it had analogies with starts I'd worked on earlier. If you cast your mind around for *analogies*, as in the general method, you get very helpful insights. I drew Fig. 23.

It was extremely fortunate that running slowly and running across both contributed to the pass – to its accuracy and its power respectively. It also meant that our fullback could, running fast, cover maybe twice as much ground as our stand-off – which gave us more flexibility with his start point. We could hide him away behind the centres. But what angle did we want him running on? Fig 24(a)

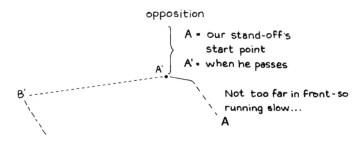

Fig 23 Letting stand-off hold the ball

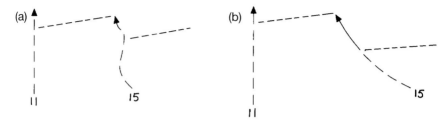

Fig 24 Getting the angle of run for the fullback
(a) This line gets him in front of the centres faster but keeps him close to opponents . . .
(b) This line takes longer to get him in front of the centres but it takes both him and wing away from defenders . . .

and (b) followed. It looked as if Fig. 24(a) would be better – it had him running away from the outside centre, and putting the winger clear of the cover. The winger, of course, would have to run off the fullback, but that presented no problems at all: we could fix it on the pitch within four runs. So we got the fullbacks running on to the pass in that direction, at virtually their top speed, with the winger coming from deep to take a long flat pass from them. The big question was whether they'd all be happy with the arrangements. Luckily, they were. If not we'd have had to work out a compromise that they could accept.

This is another key idea – compromises or *trade-offs* are the way we reconcile different needs throughout our life. This time it might have been a balance between the coach's idea of best form and the fullback's idea of comfort and confidence. But a different one was in the offing: how to arrange the centres' running in an effective compromise with the needs of the fullback. Getting good trade-offs is at the heart of coaching.

It's tied up with the idea of *priorities*. Here, for example, we've concentrated on getting an efficient strike – fullback and winger racing into space after such a pass as the opposition have never seen before. We want to compromise that as little as possible, since it's the principal element in what we're setting up.

By this time Fig. 25 was on paper. It shows our assumed set up for the actual strike – the one we'd already practised. It also shows the problem facing us: as it stands, the centres can run only about half as far as the fullback. They can't cross the line of pass, and they mustn't impede the run by the fullback. What's the best compromise we can reach in their case?

If we're going to solve it whilst retaining the work already done, we'll have to do it by altering one or some combination of the factors in their running: start position, direction of run, time of start, or speed.

The easiest answer is the last one: all we have to do is get them to run at half-speed, and the diagram will make sense. But will our centres be enough of a threat to fix the opposing centres? Provide a viable alternative if the opposition drift to cover the fullback?

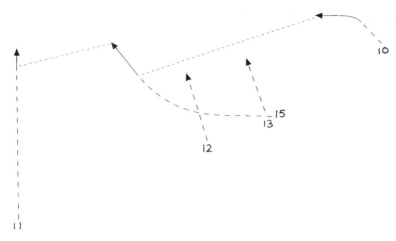

Fig. 25 **Bringing in the centres**

These are real questions, raised because backs running slowly are creating time for the opposing cover defence to reinforce the pressure defence. But the lads can try it and see how it feels.

The second-last certainly offers possibilities: if the centres had only half the time to reach the line of pass that the fullback has, then they'd be running at the same speed. So the scrum-half gets the stand-off and fullback running, and the centres start to run as the fullback reaches outside centre. But the fullback would look very obvious, wouldn't he? Still, the set up would be quite confusing to the opposition, we can try it out and see how it goes.

How about line of run? Can we find ways of having the centres run approximately the same distance as fullback? After a bit of sketching, I end up with fig. 26, which looks interesting, but would make it too easy for the opposing

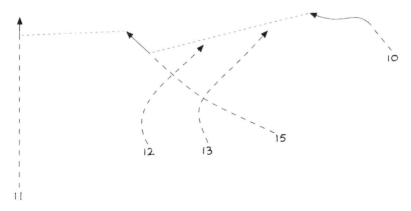

Fig 26 **Making the centres look dangerous**

outside-centre to go for the fullback and leave his own man to the cover defence. But if we rotate the diagram about 45 degrees we get a more interesting possibility, with the centres posing a very real threat. Suitably amended, it looks like Fig. 27. This isn't a finished plan, of course: it's a working sketch to give us a basic model, which we can put together more precisely in practice.

Looking at Fig. 27, you can see that some compromises have been made in the original setup for the strikers. The fullback has straightened a little; the pass from stand-off is going a little deeper. But these are exactly the kind of thing to be sorted out in practice. And I feel much happier with this version than with any of the others. The centres are going to work within the start – they're running straight and fast – and will be effective in the *alternatives* we need to build in.

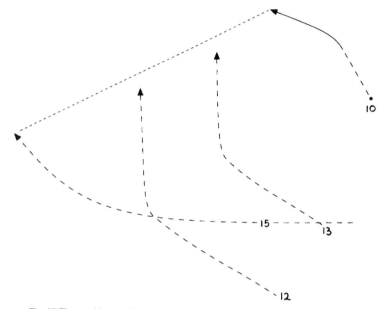

Fig. 27 **The working version**

This is a further important idea. I don't like players to get set up in isolation and find themselves being gunned down. *We want to arrange it so that the opposition has to commit itself in defence before we commit ourselves in attack.* That's the great beauty of the stand-off being able to hold the ball.

Alternatives to giving the ball to the fullback – if he's covered by a drift defence:

- we can fork their stand-off – face him with both stand-off and inside-centre, make him choose, and the other player goes for the break;

- we can give the ball to outside-centre, if their outside-centre has drifted all by himself.

And we need *support*. The kind of long spin-pass we've built this start around has one great advantage: no cover can get across that fast to defend against it. But we pay for it: none of our support cover can get across either. So the blind-side winger has to be especially aware of his duties: he has to be able to cover the outside-centre, fullback in, area. Once the fullback is in space, the breakdown will most likely be deep in their territory with their fullback tackling our winger.

I'm happy to say it all worked beautifully. Then our stand-off broke a bone in his foot in a motorbike accident; then the winger got caught running from this start – by a fullback – and did his shoulder in; and finally the fullback missed the end of the season with a broken leg. Happily, they're all fit again. So after all that work . . . but that's the way it goes, and it was great while it lasted.

DEVELOPING A START

Build up to a start . . .
Build so that each step is easy . . .
Build so that each option is left open . . .

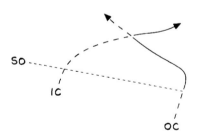

Fig. 28a **The embryonic idea**
In this first step we see a basic C3 start . . . we've got the ball wide, and opportunities may offer themselves . . .

Fig. 28b **Complication I**
We've added the IC, positioned closer to the stand-off to give a good acceleration zone, and open up other possibilities . . . intitially, they practise the switch . . .

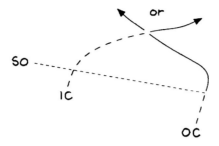

Fig. 28c Complication II

We're getting them used to a yes/no call for switch or dummy-switch . . . if it's a dummy, IC straightens . . .

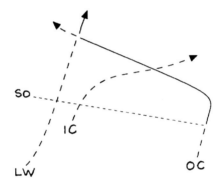

Fig. 28d Complication III

Once OC and IC are happy, we introduce our other character, in this case, LW. The idea is to get the opposing defence worried about OC and IC, whilst LW is our concealed striker. But all the options are still open: OC can take it back to the forwards; IC can take it out; LW can run it through. . . .

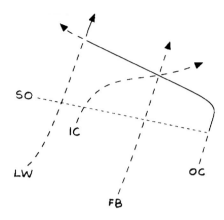

Fig. 28e **Getting support for the striker**

We turn our attention to support the LW. It's never a bad idea to move the ball out immediately the break is made, since the initial striker is that much closer to the cover, and may have lost his sense of their position in making the break. We have IC in the area, straightening, and we need to work on his positioning, to let him accelerate parallel to the LW. But that won't always be easy, so we begin to look at the role of the FB. We need a timing device that will let him appear running fast, more or less level with LW, as soon as LW has broken through into space. We need to experiment with initial position, and with starting time.

Finally, when everyone is happy and confident, we invite the back row to have a look. The scrum-half will already have done so. We think about support for OC; support behind LW; cover for FB, and work out how to meet these needs.

But if we end like that it may leave the wrong impression – of putting-off complexity. Start with something simple: it's that first step that does the trick, and gets you used to the idea of devising something original. Here's a suggestion that may help, and bring immediate results.

Referees have much relaxed the law covering the release of the ball after the tackle. Being able to keep the ball alive in the tackle – getting it safely away to the supporter – is one key to sustained open play, which e.g. in open forward attack is a most potent form of making ground and sucking in defenders.

Take the cyclic exercise described on page 53 of *Total Rugby*. 'Number four players 1–2–3–4. No. 1 has the ball and sets off at a trot from the goal line towards the 22, with the rest following in single file. No. 2 tackles him, and 1 makes the ball available on the ground. No. 3 picks up, and passes to 4' . . . and the cycle continues.

It's a great exercise – but how do you adapt it to take advantage of the new relaxation of the law? Imagine it, probe the difficulties, then get out (e.g. with your back row and scrum-half) and experiment.

10 **Enterprising back play**

Attack in Channel One affects everyone, no matter what the major strategy is. It's of major importance for the following reasons:

- It's the quickest way of getting the ball in front of the forwards and starting the most powerful form of attack – the pack handling.

- It's the way – for example by kicking – of putting the ball into the area where it's easy for us to attack, and easiest for us to defend.

- It offers the most immediate chance of a 2 v 1 against an isolated defender.

- It forms a natural continuation of attacks in the other channels, continuing in the same direction and going forward fast.

- If offers varied possibilities of developing attacks using backs and forwards (see 'enterprise in the forwards', page 185 ff.).

But:

- be sure you've enough space to justify attack (most blind-side attacks, for example, fail – if they do – for lack of space);

- be sure you attack limited space from as far forward as possible. The more space you have the easier it is to switch attackers from deeper positions (for example the stand-off switching sides at a scrum);

- attack to the blind-side has to be slick; if something delays you, fall back on your provisional alternative;

- if you're using this channel to work your way upfield, do it with players running into space rather than ploughing forward through the opposition – unless you're quite sure you can dominate and demoralise them.

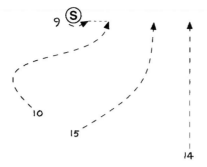

***Fig. 29* Typical attack to blind using timing device**
9 does just enough to check blind flanker. 9 has three different possible receivers. Where does he look?

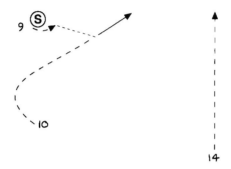

***Fig. 30* Typical attack when 10 is quick and has opened up space on the right**
Again the time device is used, with 9 doing just enough to check left flanker.

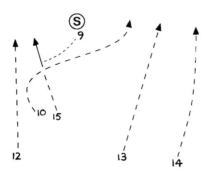

***Fig. 31* Alternative when 10's strike into the blind has been used, and his movement displaces 10 in defence**
15 runs as stand-off at moment established in practice, with 12, to fork their 13. 10 runs flat to stay onside. Why is it more effective against split centres?

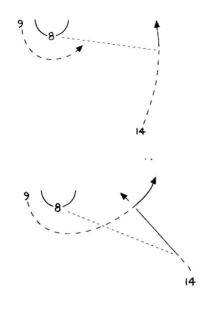

Fig. 32 No. 8 acts as scrum-half
This brings right wing into play with 9 ready to support on the inside.

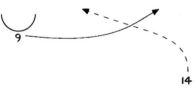

Fig. 33 No. 8 acts as scrum-half
This brings 14 into play, who runs at back row, and switches with 9.

Fig. 34 On the opposing line, the dummy-switch between 9 and 14 is very nearly a certain scorer

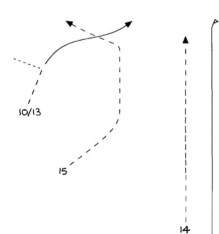

Fig. 35 An easy attack to set up, but difficult to counter
15 cuts back in where he sees a threat from the opposing back row, 10 accelerates away as he changes direction.

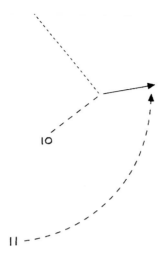

***Fig. 36* 10 runs slowly on to ball (i.e. it's put nearer to him) and swings across**
11 begins his run by moving across so that he can pick his spot for switch or
short pass. Advantages: margin for safety, change of pace.

Both of these starts allow a miss to 13, 10 shows the ball to extra man, then
spins it to OC or FB.

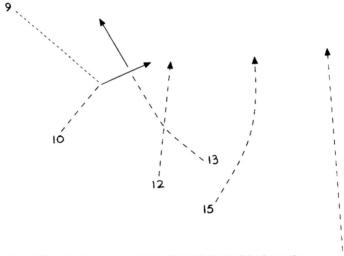

***Fig. 37* Suicide mission to get the ball back in front of the forwards**
10 runs on slowly (i.e. pass is nearer to him); he swings flat to delay pressure and
give safety margin. 12 and 15 expect a pass if 13 doesn't arrive. 13 has to enjoy
the physical side of the game.

ATTACK IN CHANNEL TWO

Attack in Channel Two is the strike in the centre – but not necessarily by your centres. It's going up against one of the hardest tackling sections of the opposition defence, so it's got to be carefully thought out, unless you've a tank-like centre prepared to drive into the tackler and take him backward, intent not on a break but on setting up a good rucking position.

- Look at the possibility of overloading them with extra players moving slowly and looking for space as they come up. Stand-off holds the ball as long as he comfortably can or needs to. But if you do this prepare to accelerate hard away from the cover.

- Worry them with chips over the top – but make sure conditions are right. It will work if:
(a) their back row are suspicious of your back row, and so a bit slow to get across – do it after we've had a go up front;
(b) the wind is behind you, and their fullback is a bit deeper than he'd like.

- Take the ball to meet them, opening up space behind. Have the centres up flat, and kick for one of them: make sure that it is precise.

- Perturb them by luring them forward, and going for the break when they're close. There's no advantage, other than possible intimidation, in running from way back. Get your stand-off going forward, swinging flat, and the first centre slicing through inside his man from close quarters. After that it's up to him to dance, and it's up to our back row to get in behind him and inside him. The probable tackle will be from the inside, and that's how he will turn.

- You can do the same with the blind-side wing, the fullback and the outside-centre, provided you set it up properly. The aim is to have lured them close *as your striker takes the switch pass*.

- Check them by striking inside them – especially if they're starting to drift. Attack their stand-off with stand-off and inside-centre, or bring your fullback or outside-centre through. Look at the diagrams and be sure you understand the running speed and angle of the stand-off.

- If their pressure is getting to you, encourage the back row to run against them – not into space as they would if they were going for scores – and bury them.

- Or split them, and keep them split whenever you can. They're strong *together* – get one isolated and have a go at him on his own.

- Early on get the stand-off to hold the ball long enough for you to check how they come up – are they together or does one lead? – before he kicks it. If one leads, get the ball to one man inside him and run in behind him to pass to *his* man.

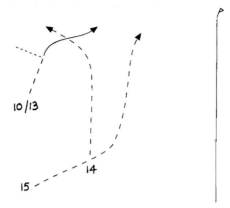

***Fig. 38* A variation on fig. 35, adding the appearance of the fullback in a less likely role**

15 starts on signal; 14 as 15 reaches him.

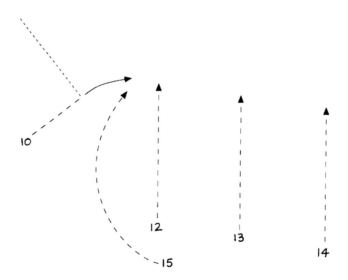

***Fig. 39* 10 runs on slowly (i.e. ball is put nearer him) and swings across looking for 15**

15 starts on signal and is running for space behind their pressure drift defence.
Advantages: margin for safety; change of pace.

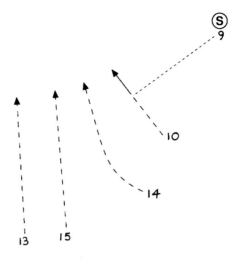

Fig. 40 10 runs on to the ball slowly, so that he can hold ball

14 and 15 are there to force opposing 10 and 12 to commit themselves. 10 (moving slow) tries to let them commit themselves first, and gives the ball to whoever is free.

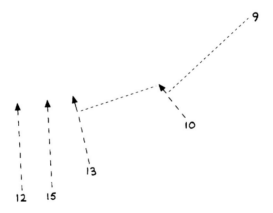

Fig 41 One of those very simple starts in which 10, 13, 15 and 12 all run gently

10 gives the ball at once to 13 hanging back, so that 13 can hold the ball while opposing 12 and 13 commit themselves. Whoever isn't covered gets the ball, and changes pace.

This is the kind of start that may well get you past the pressure defence, but it does so by slowing everything down – and that gives time for the opposition cover to get across. But it's well worth trying. 11 should be hanging back, ready to inject pace.

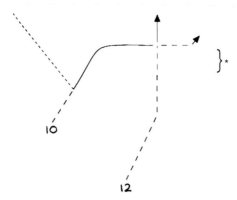

Fig. 42 Judge the point of turn to lure the opposition forward*
Use the magic square. 12 runs with 10 till he changes direction – and then 12 runs dead straight, preparing to dance his way through.

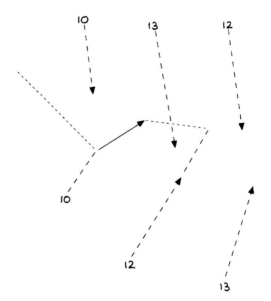

Fig. 43 Opposing 13 comes up too fast in defence
Man (in this case stand-off) runs in behind and gets the ball away fast.

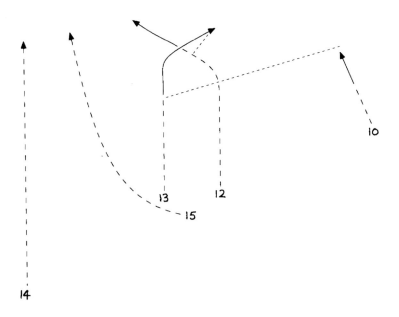

Fig. 44 Think of this as a switch

The timing is important – commit yourselves after the opposition are committed.

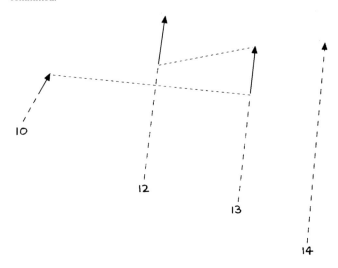

Fig. 45 To be used when the opposing defence is committed to getting wide quickly

ATTACK IN CHANNEL THREE

This form of attack is the most expansive in rugby, involves the most players, offers the best entertainment. It seeks to exploit the space on the fringes of the defence by using speed and skill.

- The problem is not one of getting the ball there:
  (a) if your stand-off makes adequate space by taking the ball deep;
  (b) if you use a miss – preferably mixing misses from stand-off to outside-centre with misses from inside-centre to fullback or wing;
  (c) if the only player to hold the ball is the player on the inner edge of the channel, i.e. who gives the ball to the actual striker; and
  (d) if your team literally spins the ball – then you can be sure of getting the ball wide.

- The problem is preventing the opposition from drifting. In effect this means that instead of trying to pressure your midfield trio, the opposing midfield trio are shifting out so that their outside-centre is running into Channel Three, and filling the gap.

  Most teams do this from line-out; comparatively few do it from scrums: you should seek to spin the ball wide from scrums. The orthodox opinion that you should move the ball wide from line-outs and only from line-outs is rubbish. By the time you get the ball wide at line-outs – unless you've built in a deterrent – the opposition defence will be waiting for you. If it is, the best thing to do is to kick deep down the open touch from outside-centre. If they start drifting from scrums, you concentrate on attacking their stand-off with your stand-off and inside-centre: your stand-off holds the ball, forcing their stand-off to choose between his pressure target (stand-off) and drift target (inside-centre); whoever he doesn't choose becomes the striker, running diagonally into space.

- All kicking for a particular channel is best done from the inside edge of that channel. Channel Three is no exception: the most effective attacking kicks are from the outside-centre into the area behind the opposing winger – who will already have started to move up – and behind and away from the cover whose first target will have been the handling attack. You kick down touch; your winger gets between touch and the ball; your outside-centre covers the opposing fullback. Kicking from inside-centre offers an acceptable trade-off against pressure.

- Where play starts on the edge of Channel Three, all the same ideas about kicking apply – but we're now looking at the most effective of all kicks – the chip into the box. This should always be a live possibility to both scrum-half and blind winger from any scrum, on, say, the 15m line. If there's space (and after reading this book, let's hope the scrum-half is consciously looking for that space) behind the winger, it's on.

- The player passing to the intended striker should carry the ball as far as possible before giving the pass: this imposes the greatest strain on the cover defence, who have to shift target late.

- Once the ball is in the striker's hands, he's going forward trying to preserve space outside him, and determined that the ball won't die. He should have a variety of passes he can use to keep the ball alive, whetted in intensive handling practices.

- Using the width of the field doesn't give the best odds, but it does give space to use the two obvious strikers – the fullback and the blind-side wing. Think of them as twin fullbacks to be used interchangeably whenever we're reasonably sure of getting the ball at a tactical point. Use them as extra men; use them as diversions to check the opposition defence. They're almost certainly two of your best runners: use them. But use them when you're confident that you won't make unforced errors – that your skill levels make the risks of using them in attack acceptable.

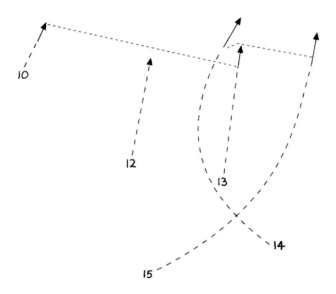

Fig 46 15 and 14 both start on signal . . . 13 gives it to either in space

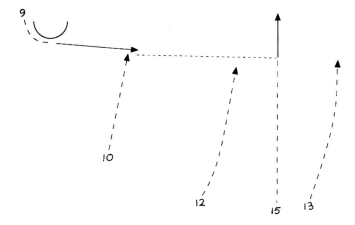

***Fig. 47* The timing of this is more critical than when 12 holds the ball, swings sideways and feeds 14 when he appears**

9 moves backwards slightly to give more time for the runners. He dummies a switch to 10 and fires the ball across 12 to 15. 12 and 13 keep the channel open.

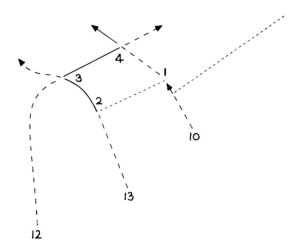

***Fig. 48* 10 runs on slowly, passes, checks**

13 is close and lying back – he runs on to the pass, already heading out to speed the switch. 12 running straight comes back quickly for the switch, and concentrates on 2nd switch. 10 waits, then accelerates into switch. 13 should be hanging back ready to support.

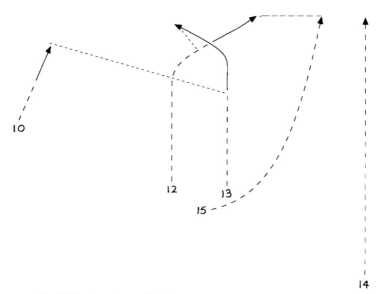

Fig. 49 **Simple and very effective**

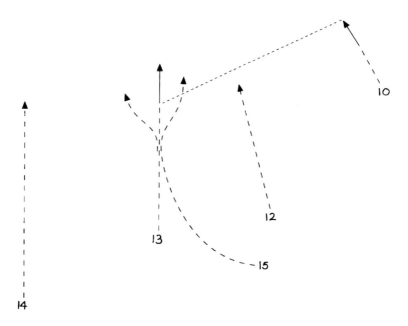

Fig. 50 **Too often 15 commits himself before he needs to**
Get behind outside-centre and call 'in' or 'out' as you run for space.

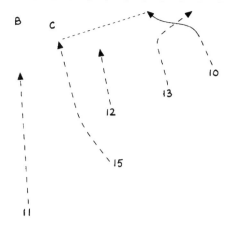

Fig. 51 15/11 start on signal

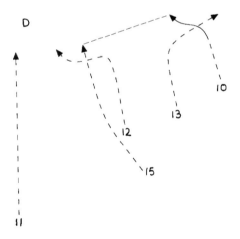

Fig. 52 Here's the same start with 12 looping to be outside 15 when the ball arrives

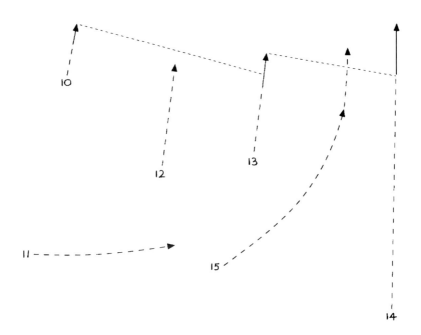

Fig. 53 **A double miss to get the ball wide fast – more probably with right-hand passes**

15 remains available as support on the inside.

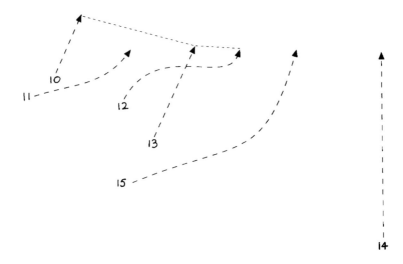

Fig. 54 **11 comes in to check the centres, while 12 loops outside 13 before 13 gets the ball**

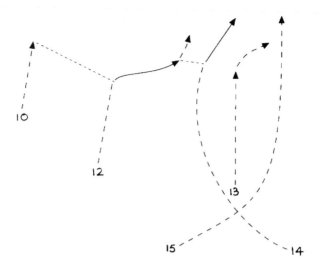

Fig 55 **Simple but effective**
The key is the movement sideways by 12, which creates a safety margin for 14 and a change of pace.

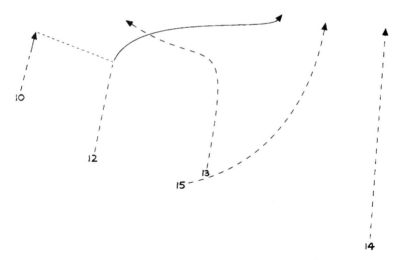

Fig 56 **The key to this consistently successful start is that 12 and 13 go forward together to the point where the opponents find it hard to respond**
Both run flat – that's what lets 15 hit the line at speed.

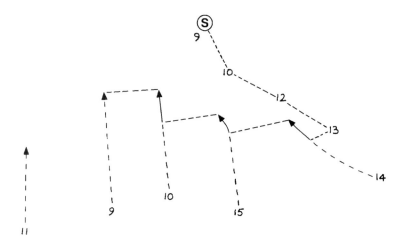

Fig 57 10 lies a little deeper and more behind scrum to facilitate movement back into line

9 passes and runs. Both 9 and 10 work hard to get deep. 10 standing passes to 12 standing, who passes to inside shoulder of 13 standing. As 12 passes, 14 sets off running under cover of 12 to receive ball. He's accompanied by 15. You then attack the wide channel your positioning has cleared on the left.

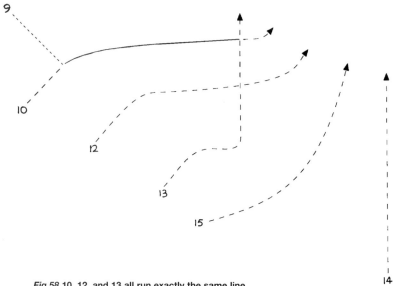

Fig 58 10, 12, and 13 all run exactly the same line

13 straightens when he sees space, and the magic square ensures he's running fast and straight as he takes the ball.

There's something to be said for reserving carrying moves for movement to the right, and miss moves for movement to the left.

11 Enterprising forward play

Effective forward play depends to a large extent on close integration. There are three factors in securing that integration.

(i) Forward drills in practices

This is the basic method of establishing uniformity of aim and method among the forwards. Immediate actions in a pressure situation need an instantaneous reaction akin to those in hand-to-hand fighting, and that kind of reaction comes from intensive repetition practices. In the instant, a speed of response is needed that could only be slowed by conscious thought. In other situations (for example line-outs), the need for immediate reaction is modified by the need to co-ordinate with a set plan; and in yet others – once possession has been established at scrum or maul, for example – it is replaced by a much more conscious manipulation of the situation, though this again is solidly based on practical experience. Typically, forward integration tends to be least effective in loose play where judgement is clearly required but most coaches have no means of supplying it.

(ii) The forward leader

It's customary to spend some time choosing a forward leader, but virtually none on defining his job. He can normally be said to have two functions:

(a) to keep morale high, by action and word: *the motivator*; and

(b) to make sure, by action and word, that team policy is implemented, and to correct technical/organisation faults: *the coach on the field*.

Whilst ideally he should be able to react to the unexpected and produce a method of countering it, it's more realistic to see his function in terms of maintaining established form. It always pays to put him solidly in charge of forward practices, so that he gains a coaching insight.

(iii) The tactical leader

This, too, is often regarded as a function of the forward leader. In a limited sense, some tactical decisions fit into category (ii) (b) above: they are the implementation of team policy, and represent less a decision than the reinforcement of a habit.

For example, it ought to be team policy to move the ball to the back of the maul immediately it's won, and the pack leader's reminders of this reinforce the tactical point. This highlights his need for constant alertness, and a grasp of the unit repertoire analogous to those of the TDM.

But inevitably any of the forwards will tend to find himself frequently in situations where he lacks the field of view to be able to formulate decisions on the use of the ball. There's a strong case for delegating this tactical leadership to the scrum-half, who is close enough to recognise the comparative strengths of the packs, and who is so placed that at virtually all scrums, line-outs, rucks and mauls he can see exactly what the opposing defence is doing both close to the point and further afield.

The position in which the pack leader plays is secondary to his qualities as a leader and analyst, but, other things being equal, there's a lot to be said for his functioning at No. 8 – on the same spinal column as the halves and FB, a loose forward with strong affinities to the front five, and a player inevitably involved in forward attacks, and in the controlled release of the ball. Indeed, he may often, and will more frequently, I think, in future, function as an auxiliary scrum-half.

The No. 8's abilities and inabilities affect the options open to the team in the same way as those of the halves, though to a lesser extent. It pays, therefore, to give him a little extra attention.

Controlling the feed

He's in position to control the feed of the ball to the scrum-half. He must understand the basic needs of timing: release/feed the ball as soon as the scrum-half calls for it, and only when he calls for it; and understand the two-stage timing system, in which he counts the necessary moments for the scrum-half to get into position.

Technically this is not difficult. He can control the ball with knees or feet. It pays to have him practise both in his normal position and in Channel One, where if the scrum is under pressure he can function usefully both in feeding and in setting up attacks to the left.

Feeding the scrum-half

This is useful when the scrum-half wants to pass left without pressure, or to the right after a wheel; when he's going for a long kick; when he's slightly slow in getting the ball away.

It's as well to remember that though this takes the pressure off the scrum-half, it slows the ball movement, and increases pressure in midfield. It shouldn't be done as a matter of course.

The mechanics are fairly straightforward:

- left foot forward to support weight;
- locate the ball-receiver;
- check whether it's to be taken standing or moving (this will normally be clear from practice);
- try to get ball well forward and slightly to the right;
- practise continuous push from first contact with ball, and keep left shoulder low as you pivot clockwise to feed.

'Scrum-half' is shorthand for a variety of receivers. There's no reason why the right flanker or the right wing shouldn't be the receiver. Most players can learn to perform a fine scrum-half pass very fast following the sequence in *Total Rugby*, and it pays to have all of your back row acquire the ability. The No. 8 pass can come that much quicker, with your regular scrum-half standing waiting as for a feed to distract and so reinforce the surprise.

Whether your No. 8 can employ these abilities, or the ability to initiate an attack from the tight by a personal attack, depends on the performance of the players in front of him. Everything is easy if we have the initiative, but may become impossible if the No. 8 is under pressure. One of the things that the No. 8 should be telling the scrum-half – at the start of the match, and as soon as he detects any significant change – is the kind of pressure that's on him. The scrum-half needs this information to understand what's on in terms of breaks and of controlling the timing for gambits in the backs.

Equally, if he launches a back-row attack, the performance of the rest of the pack in its support running is an excellent indicator of success or failure. The main reasons for the failure of back-row moves are often to be found in the front five.

One obvious step the coach can take, therefore, in improving the chances for the No. 8, is to improve the speed of heel, and so reduce the period under pressure before the No. 8 starts. If the scrum-half has called early so that the pack know what's on, that may call forth a greater concentration of effort. For what's needed is concentration on good established form. If the coach has coached properly, has drilled them in their scrumming, and they apply themselves conscientiously, they should reach something like their maximum output.

The scrum-half calls early, has the ball ready, gets it in as fast as the hooker signals. The pack get there first, get bound first, with weight forward ready to engage as one man when the hooker sees the four heads, drives forward and up, with the hooker ready positioned, and the channels clear, and drives straight as the hooker's foot moves. We all know what's wanted, and as coaches our job is to exact it from the players.

The No. 8 has to be efficient so that he operates fast as soon as the signal comes. He may hold the ball for good reasons:

- the scrum-half doesn't signal: because there's accidental delay; because he's adjusting the tempo; because he's controlling the timing;
- the No. 8 is trying to lure the opposition into thinking a back-row attack is imminent so that opponents don't concentrate on pushing, and simplify the secondary drive.

But this kind of intentional delay is utterly unlike the delay resulting from faulty technique.

The pressure must be kept on the opposing pack from the moment the scrummage starts to a moment or two after the back-row attack starts: it's fatal for the pressure to slacken as the rest of the pack prepare to support the attack that's about to start.

But as soon as the attack is under way, it needs support, and, tired or not, the rest of the pack must give it. You should welcome fatigue; it gives your superior fitness and commitment the best chance to pay off.

For the coach, the overall need once the start is established as an effective technique is to present it to the players as part of a sequence of scrum . . . attack . . . support, in which each part is equally important and demands equal commitment.

TACTICAL DECISION-MAKING FOR THE BACK-ROW ATTACK

This is typical of the kind of situation in which the scrum-half takes over as decision-maker. He in functioning all the time as a team member responsible for personal decisions, but respecting the tactical calls of the stand-off. If he sees an immediate advantage, he is free to exploit it. If he is successful, he's a good player; if he's not, and yet persists, the coach has to intervene and make sure he recognises team priorities.

In the period before deciding to launch a back-row attack, the scrum-half is quietly assessing the basic conditions that allow the attack: the balance between the packs in the tight, and the quality of the opposing back row. He chooses to launch an attack from the back of the scrum either because he's happy on those conditions, or because he sees a need to relieve pressure elsewhere, or both.

He's then waiting for a promising situation to present itself. He'll have been prepared for this by extensive experience, in practice, of what the pack needs to carry out a particular attack. The coach may well have employed back-row attack as a theme for unopposed, showing the range of attacks appropriate to particular situations.

The first determinant of his choice is:

Space

(a) How much space is there?

There are some types of attack that can be made when there appears to be no space at all; others require, or function best in, a lot. The scrum-half will have an idea of the move he wants to try, and be waiting for the right space to appear. If he's being pressured into trying attacks to relieve pressure elsewhere, the length of his wait will depend on the variety of the unit repertoire, and his confidence in them.

(b) How do we get good angles of run?

As far as possible, forwards should be trying to run straight upfield. You can imagine a forward running across to set up a switch, but it's not something to be encouraged indiscriminately. 'Go forward' is a fine precept for every forward. So, it's pointless launching a back-row attack to the right from a wheeled scrum: it's not going to work. If you're wheeled, and you need to attack short, you're better taking on the opposing scrum-half and flanker on the left than running across. And if you have practised from that situation, there's no reason why it shouldn't work.

(c) Have the backs made space for us?

As a good situation approaches, the scrum-half calls early – to concentrate the pack, to allow the players to rehearse their actions, and to let the stand-off improve the available space. He does this by:

- positioning his centres on the side away from the projected attack, and pushing the winger wide; and
- preparing dummy movement to distract the defence.

Both of these will have been worked on in practice.

(d) How much ground do we need to make?

Some forms of attack are extremely effective in terms of a short-term gain: they'll let you go forward 3m – but they won't let you set up a long-range attack. Others are more flexible, but perhaps less certain over a few metres. This is one reason why back-row moves, like penalties, are best thought of closely linked to particular situations on the pitch. We can reduce the load on the scrum-half by working out answers to these questions for our team, by building up our repertoire, making it efficient, and linking it to given situations. But the scrum-half has to understand the thinking, and contribute to it.

Overload

If you've the right No. 8 he may be an overload on his own – fast and strong enough to drive forward and score over a short distance, or to keep possession and get the ball back when he's stopped. But most coaches don't possess that kind of player. What they're looking for is some kind of numerical advantage to put a player into space.

Much of the effort in designing back-row moves goes into securing the extra man. What we're looking for is something like:

2 v 1 . . . . . . No. 8 + scrum-half	v	flanker
scrum-half + flanker	v	flanker
3 v 2 . . . . . . No. 8 + scrum-half + flanker	v	flanker + No. 8

Your chances of getting these depend partly on the system your opponents are playing. They may have their No. 8 intent on getting across for the extra man in the backs; partly on their efficiency – their No. 8 may be very slow to get his head up; partly on the weaknesses imposed upon them by your staple activity – their back row may be forced to start very fast across field to cover your overlap attack.

But you must consider, too, the possibility of linking the back row start to a development by the backs, with the fullback or stand-off functioning as the real striker. This adds the advantage of a change of pace to the advantage of extra players. However, to do this effectively you need to be able to control the timing of the various starts.

The third determinant is:

Surprise

Surprise comes in two forms:

1. your opponents don't see what's coming: speed and the unexpected;

2. what they think is coming doesn't: diversion and deception.

1. Speed of execution is essential in all rugby. The speed you can play at is a function of your technical expertise: you play within it, and you seek to improve it. If speed becomes haste, and haste leads to inaccuracy, the whole action becomes slow; play within your capability, and register the need to improve your capability.

The unexpected comes in various forms. As always, it helps you think about and devise new versions of them if you categorise them.

Unexpected positions or movement

This is what most people probably think of first. It is of course, difficult to produce a whole line of new gambits, but a few starts which are new are outlined in fig. 59.

Unexpected aggression

Many teams accustomed to winning through forward power expect no challenge close to the scrum. (The same thing, incidentally, is true of teams playing very enterprising rugby: they aren't accustomed to teams who run the ball at them and their defence is comparatively untested.) There is a potential advantage in taking them on, not directly, but close to their power. A further advantage, if it's done early, is that the close attack may affect their commitment simply to out-scrumming the lighter team: the back row have something else to think about.

Unexpected skills

Another assumption we can turn to our advantage is that a forward is limited in his running and passing skills. This is reinforced by those quasi-official definitions of the skill needed for particular positions – definitions that limit props to giving short passes! This means that the opposition don't expect miss-passes, switches, over-the-shoulder passes, and so on. If we can build up this kind of ability, it means that at least in the short term we can take them by surprise. And equally, the ability and desire to elude the tackler and run the ball forward will come as a surprise.

This is particularly valuable in designing short penalty moves: if you've a forward who can do a genuine spin-pass – and they should all be able to do that – you can shift the focus of attack decisively. And if, instead of running into opponents, your forwards can wrong-foot them, you can penetrate their first line of defence.

Another useful instance comes at the No. 8 break from the scrum. If he's got two men (for example scrum-half and flanker, or scrum-half and stand-off, or scrum-half and wing) outside him, he can disrupt the opposing flanker's preparations by doing a miss to the outside supporter.

Unexpected possession

Taking the ball against the head, provided we get a quick heel, is an excellent springboard for close attack. We must have a policy decision on how we're going to use it, so that we can move straight into action and use the precious moments of reaction in the opposition. If we get that fast heel, I feel the best bet is a fast flat break by the scrum-half out to the left, checking the opposition with dummies to stand-off and centre, and looking for a 2 v 1 with our outside-centre against their outside-centre. It's far better, of course, if our fullback can run from deep to link with him, but it depends greatly on his positioning at the opposition put-in.

2. The second category of surprise covers *diversion and deception*. It resembles the art of the conjuror, who distracts his audience from the essential action with an impressive but irrelevant flourish. Indeed, it's possible to do just that: commit yourself to one action, and set out to disguise it. That's acceptable if you have what you think is a sure-fire strike. However, as a general rule, it's better to think of this situation in terms of committing yourself last: allowing the opponent to choose, and then doing the other. So all your players accept that, whether they're likely to get the ball or not, they must expect it: their run is for real, if the ball comes their way.

The alternative attack then is likely to involve the backs, who have the intention of wrong-footing the defence, drawing players out of position. It's the second stage of their attempt to make the forward attack more successful by their positioning – making sure that the forwards can move forward into space.

The other main variety of deception is the repetition of a start, with a different development. This is a specific case of a general rule: reassure the opponent before you strike. In fact, any start with only one development is weak. It suggests that the coach has inhibited his players by programming their activity, rather than creating a situation they can exploit from their personal skills. It's good to end the gambit with players running on lines that allow alternative development. At a certain stage, you may find it convenient to suggest and work through alternative developments: if *that's* not on, do *this*. But to see the start as exactly that – a prelude to put players at an advantage which they then exploit in an open-ended way – is in the long term a better bet. It does suggest, of course, the value of attending to the extension and refinement of personal skills.

I've already suggested that:

- we need to establish the start by intensive work within the unit paying attention to the preceding scrum, and final support;
- we need to build it into team preparations so that the backs can think about their clearing of space and alternative diversion/attack.

This team preparation may well be covered in thematic unopposed, with back-row attack as the theme. Briefly, the coach must recognise that, like penalties, different points on the field, with varying distances to go forward, and space to work in, require different forms of back-row attack. He should move round the field, therefore, playing the attack, continuing through second phase with the TDM dictating, then switching to another point, up and down the pitch, till the team recognises what's likely to work.

The starts in Fig. 59 on page 193 lead to a variety of close attacks, which can be as programmed or as open-ended as the coach thinks fit. The great beauty about the open-ended approach is that it prepares the players to meet the unexpected in the match – not to expect too much, and to make the most of what there is.

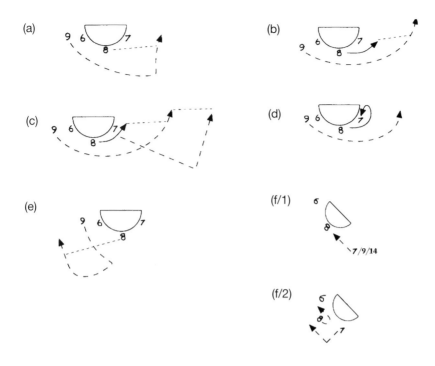

Fig. 59 Typical starts for a back-row attack

The coach has to balance the need for a varied attack against the need for simplicity. It's better to have very few starts the unit know intimately than a dozen still on the drawing board.

Of course, if the back row and scrum-half are a major strike force in your team, it pays to develop their repertoire, and to tailor the use of the ball by the backs to suit them: they need a back strike close enough to them to give good running lines, and you need to work on getting them a little further back in the time they tend to stand and wait for the attack to reach them: the deeper they are, the sooner they can support, and the faster their running speed. But essentially they need to be able to turn as many situations as possible into attack possibilities. As in Fig. 59 above, we might categorise these as:

(i)	scrum under pressure	a, scrum-half alone, b
(ii)	partially wheeled scrum	f/1, f/2
(iii)	non-wheeled scrum	all except f/1, f/2
(iv)	where space is available	b, c
(v)	where very limited space is available	d, f/2
(vi)	on their line	d, scrum-half/winger

For teams less adapted to close attack, and while building up the full repertoire, it pays to identify those situations you are particularly likely to meet, or need to exploit, and make sure that you cover them before paying excessive attention to any one in particular. It's pointless having four ways of attacking space on the right, if you're sure you're going to be wheeled on a high percentage of your put-ins.

(i) SCRUM UNDER PRESSURE

If that pressure is too great, back-row attack may not be on. If the pressure is very great, it may be better to use Channel One and get the ball out quickly. If this causes emotional or technical stress to your scrum-half, you should try shifting your No. 8 to the space between left flanker and left lock, where he can control the ball, and feed.

If you can attack close (or to the left), it may distract the opposition from their eight-man shove. It's worth considering early on before the pressure takes full effect.

The easiest start will be the scrum-half going himself. This allows complete commitment from all eight in the pack. Where he goes depends on his own talent: if he's quick he should go flat and then forward; if he's big, and can take on the opposing back row, he can go close. It's idle trying one when you should be trying the other.

A better bet in terms of the running line of the scrum-half is (b) – the feed from No. 8, after the scrum-half has dropped out wider and deeper. The scrum-half doesn't move from that position till he sees the ball in the No. 8's hands. He must run on to a flattish pass, and the lead must be established in practice. Of course, for at least a moment, the No. 8 can't exert full power in the scrummage.

It's evident that if the scrum is under severe pressure, then some of the starts are non-starters. It's as important to recognise what isn't on as what is: in many ways, the very good player is one who doesn't try what's not on. Under pressure, the tight-head prop needs as much help as possible from the flank and the hooker. The hooker, as soon as he has struck and checked the strike is clean, should be squeezing tight to the tight-head, and giving him all the help he can. And every player in the pack should be thinking 'right shoulder' against the incipient wheel.

We've already looked at the general need for greater speed based on greater efficiency as the key requirement for lessening the impact of the pressure.

(ii) WHEELED SCRUM

Let's hope the law-makers outlaw the wheel – well, they nearly did – but if they don't, here's what we can do.

Prevention is better than cure, but preventing the wheel is often very difficult and sometimes impossible. The best bet is to drive into a lock, with the front row as low as the hooker's strike will allow, the hooker committed to the tight-head prop; the flanker pushing straight forward; and the whole scrum committed to a right-shoulder shove, to high efficiency and speed.

But this may not be enough; and if the opposition recognise that their push is indispensable to our lock, then all is lost. If their tight-head trio (i.e. the tight-head, right flanker and right lock) take off the pressure for a moment, our lock will be broken. Our lock only works if our players are compressed. If you imagine a stick leaning against a fence – it's not 'locked'. You have to push it down in the middle and get its base closer to the fence, so that it is exerting force, before it's locked. If the fence gives way for a moment, the lock is broken. Exactly the same is true of our pack. If you are wheeled, you can forget back-row attacks to the right. As a sound general rule, forwards should go forward. To start off running across is to invite a tackle with the resulting situation all in favour of the opposition. But the attack to the left is complicated by the presence there of the opposing scrum-half.

This is not to say that you can't attack to the right. Once the wheel is on, the opposing back row are pretty well committed. The left flanker and the No. 8 are in danger of breaking too early and being offside, so they tend to be cautious. The right flanker is covering the right side in case of a break-out. If we can get a feed to scrum-half, and a quick pass to our stand-off going right, he may not have to worry at all about their back row. Equally, we may be able to feed our fullback in the same way.

That apart, we must examine the possibilities of attacking to the left, or at least minimising the danger by converting the wheeled scrum into a maul. Perhaps that's too negative a way of looking at it. There was a time when the pack in possession would engineer a wheel, would set out to create it. The thinking is clear enough: if we can get their pack out from between us and the opposition line, the way is clear to attack. I remember that venerable figure, Adrian Stoop, writing to me enclosing a Harlequin hand-out from the late 1920s giving technical details of how to wheel as a means of creating attacking opportunities.

The danger now with the revised laws is less the completely disruptive wheel, than of a wheel within legitimate limits that is followed by a drive.

When this happens regularly in a match, it's sensible to shift your No. 8 to the left, to bind between flanker and lock and control Channel One. This allows your hooker to strike for the clearest, shortest channel, and so gets the ball to No. 8 faster, lessening the difficulty of opposition pressure. It also places your No. 8 in an interesting attacking position. He becomes a threat and absorbs the attention of the opposing scrum-half, and is in a better position to let the right flanker strike effectively to the left. If he is powerful enough, your No. 8 can pivot clockwise out of the scrum holding the ball, withstand the assault of the scrum-half, and offer the right flanker the chance of going inside (between No. 8 and scrum) or outside on his own. You'll see the possibilities of operating the second and third variations suggested in Fig. 60 in a neat and compact form. Or you can use starts f/1 and f/2 from Fig 59.

195

(i)   Start f/1. The No. 8 has the ball under control. He shouts 'defence', pauses for a second to let 7 collect himself, then picks up turning clockwise. As he does so, 7 drives in on him, left shoulder forward, so that they have four hands on the ball, and sets up a maul.

(ii) Start f/2. Near their line, 8 picks up turning clockwise to feed 7 going for the line outside him.

(iii) Start f/2. Near their line, 8 picks up, turning clockwise as if to feed 7 in (ii), then pivots anti-clockwise to drive for the line.

With these starts, even more than normally, a fast support is invaluable. It can get the bulk of our forwards past the opposite pack – a massive outflanking, which was precisely what the old time wheel was about. But it calls for great discipline to do it.

(iii) NON-WHEELED SCRUM

This considerably expands what you can do. The only one that we need to deal with is No. 5. This is an elegant and effective way of attacking the left side. You need a nippy scrum-half, and if you want to develop the attack over a distance you need to link it to a well-timed intervention by the stand-off.

The move is very simple. The scrum-half puts the ball in, follows round as normal, checks the space is still open on the left, slaps the No. 8, and moves back and wide. The No. 8 gives him enough time – established, as always, in practices – to get there, then picks up and takes a short step to the left. He must expect to need to pass at once, and you need to check angles so that he can get the ball to the scrum-half even if the flat-pass is out. Ideally, of course, we're looking for as flat a pass as he can make since it limits the opposing scrum-half's ability to intervene. But judgement comes into it: the opposing scrum-half may have moved wide to cover our one. If so, the No. 8 goes forward himself. If he's in danger of being checked, he tries to get the ball in front of our left flanker to set up a drive near the line, or a maul. The scrum-half doesn't move till he sees the ball in 8's hands.

To get maximum advantage, you want the stand-off switching from the right of the scrum (where, of course, he has positioned himself to keep the space clear on the left) to appear outside the scrum-half running fast. The timing start is from the slap. He feints right – and his centres move with him – then swings across on a curve to get outside the scrum-half. The exact delay by the No. 8 is established by trial and error in practice. If we can get him running fairly straight onto the ball it gives him the best chance of developing the attack himself, with the back row coming up on the inside.

(iv) WHERE SPACE IS AVAILABLE

Space that exists, or we've improved, or even created by the positioning of our backs, makes life much easier in the back-row attack. But to make the most of it we need an overload, and we need speed. If you take a very simple example – and a very effective move – you'll see the essentials: a start by the No. 8, with a feed to the scrum-half running into space at speed the technical aim. We don't want the scrum-half running slow as a result of not making enough depth for himself; we don't want him hauled down by the opposing No. 8 because he hasn't got wide enough; we want him choosing a line of run rather than having one imposed on him by our technical lack of expertise. We want him to have an advantage in time based on the sheer speed of our start. We've made a decision, and we have the skill in our scrumming and use of time and space to exploit it.

We can build on this start: we can think about getting our stand-off outside the scrum-half applying the same timing techniques as described in section (iii) above.

(v) WHERE VERY LIMITED SPACE IS AVAILABLE

The beauty of limited space, especially near the opposing line, is that the opposition may not believe that you can use it. There are possible back-row starts – especially start (d) – that can give you a limited but very probable gain where there appears to be no space at all. Imagine the scrum with only a couple of metres blind-side, right on the opposing line. Our winger has moved over behind the stand-off 'because there's simply no room for him'. The attack is virtually bound to go left.

But No. 8 breaks fast and close with the object of getting the ball in front of 7, and 7 then has several options: to turn completely and feed the scrum-half standing or running on to the ball: to get his head down and drive for the line; or to check for support, and then start rolling, anti-clockwise, supported by the rest of the pack. (Incidentally, if you want a tight roll, get the supporting player to put the outside arm right round the ball-carrier, so they're really tight, and the other round the ball.) In the case outlined, he's driving for the line, with 8 doing his best to help.

Of course, this move will work quite effectively where more room is available, especially if the backs look as though they're going to use that space. Say the scrum is 20m in from the right touch, and both the fullback and the stand-off swing across into that space – the back row cannot afford not to cover them, and that wrong-foots them for the tight attack. Of course, the back attack ought to function for real if required, and you'll tend to go for your strength in choosing between the attacks.

(vi) ON THEIR LINE

We've already looked at various starts that work close in. If you've a powerful No. 8 or scrum-half they can often drive forward the necessary distance. It's a question partly of technique – getting themselves into a low driving position, with their head slightly under hip-level and the ball well back, ready to roll back if they get stopped. The opponent should see the wedge of their back from shoulders to hips, and very little else. Partly, it's a matter of sheer commitment. Many players seem never to realise just how hard you can be to stop if you simply make up your mind to go and present a poor target.

A very effective attack with a little more space on the right is the dummy-switch between scrum-half and winger. The winger aims for the opposing flanker, and the scrum-half for space and the line.

On the other side of the field, start 5 can be very effective, simply because the attack to the left is unexpected, and both the f/2 attacks are hard to stop. The dummy to 7, with No. 8 pivoting inside and diving over 6's legs, uses space that doesn't exist at ground level!

Fig. 60(a)

This is the basic form. 8 has gone forward close, decided there's no chance for him, and turned in to 7. 5 and 6 join them and they set up a maul. With that maul we can attempt to move forward – slow, calm, deliberate, determined. So many forwards think that blind effort is needed in a case like this; far from it. Control is the thing.

Alternatively we can begin to roll – one hand to bind with, one for the ball – churning counter-clockwise, and looking for space.

Fig. 60(b)

The first variation is often even more effective. If the opposing 6 has gone at all wide, it's highly likely that our 7 can slide through inside. 7 can reckon the odds as soon as 8 breaks: he can see where 6 has got to, but he must be looking for it. When 7 goes, he does so in the same attitude described in the last section. He shouldn't try to roll on his back, or hold the ball aloft if he's stopped: the hands around him will probably be attached to opponents. He should simply get his shoulders lower, and push the ball gently behind him as his head approaches the ground.

In both (a) and (b) you'll see that our scrum-half has contributed to the start by going out sideways, as a potential threat.

Both (a) and (b) concentrate attack close, on the immediate right of the scrum, where attack is unexpected simply because there doesn't appear to be enough space for one. When there is space, however, we can adapt the start to let us get into it. This is best done after we've tried (a) or (b): we use the less predictable first, to create conditions in which the more predictable has an edge.

Once the opposing 6 expects a close attack from that start, we can open it out.

Fig 60(c)

In C, as soon as 8 gives him the ball, 7 is turning to face the rear. 6 and 9 are both running right. The ultimate striker must be 9, since it's very likely that 6 will come under immediate pressure – I have seen him run 40m to score, but I've seen him caught far, far, too often to suggest you trust it – so his aim, generally, is to take out one more defender by his presence, but to hand the ball on to 9 almost as he takes it himself. If you think of the first ball-carrier transferring the ball in a line-out peel, you'll get the idea. And in both cases, we face a problem of timing: there's no point in 6 or 9 starting fast, and having to slow down or stop because the ball's not available, so 6 moves back to x, where he can see developments, and he starts to run when he sees the ball in 7's hands – the basic timing device for anyone acting as 'stand-off'. 9, too, checks at x – but where exactly his x is will be determined by his relative speed: you work it out by trial and error so that he is moving at his highest possible speed as 6 hands on the ball.

Fig. 60(d)

This has the same effect, and is even more speedy in execution. In this, 8 feints to take the ball to 7, as the opposition may now expect, but as soon as he goes forward he starts pivoting to feed 9. The great thing is to get 9 running really fast,

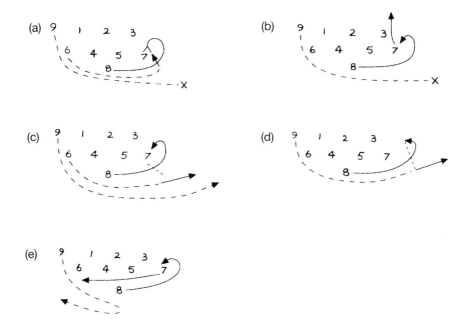

Fig 60 **Variations on a back-row attack**

which calls for fairly precise timing – only 'fairly' because 8 can pass at any time as he pivots. On the other hand, there's built-in safety: if anything goes badly wrong with the timing, 8 can drive on to 7.

9's line of run depends on the space available to him: he could be running into an empty half field, if the backs by their positioning have prepared the way for him. It may also depend on his own talents: if he's very quick, he should use his speed and get wide; if he's well balanced and durable he may try straightening earlier, and looking for support inside him.

Fig. 60(e)

This variation developed straight from a try scored by doing it when we were blocked on the right, and the scrum had slightly wheeled. The only development came in getting 9 to change direction and accompany 7 on his run. The first score came without benefit of support.

Once again, if you are setting it up, you're looking for a blindside on the left, which has been emptied of defenders other than the right wing, who has been pulled wide by our left wing. If we try it on the far right, we're going to run into defenders – stand-off and centres – that we don't really need to meet. Why not wait till the position is right? This is the core idea of 'situations' as the basis of team tactics.

Equally, you play this when 7 thinks it's right: when he's got the ball safe, when no opponent is hanging on to him, when he can see 9 and 9 nods to tell him the blind is empty. He goes the shortest way. 9 starts just before 7 reaches him and accelerates outside him for the pass or for the dummy.

Now remember: it's not likely that any team will play all these variations. Find those that suit you, and get intimate with them.

PREPARING A CO-ORDINATED ATTACK

This is an exercise for the reader. You have to work out the organisation in space, timing, and decision-making of the integrated attack by forwards and backs outlined in Fig. 61.

Space

- What prompts the coach to prepare for this situation?
- How has he improved the space available?
- How could he improve it further? (and why hasn't he?)
- Roughly how much space from scrum to touch does he need?
- Roughly how close to the goal-line does the scrum have to be?
- When 9 takes up position who should see his front?

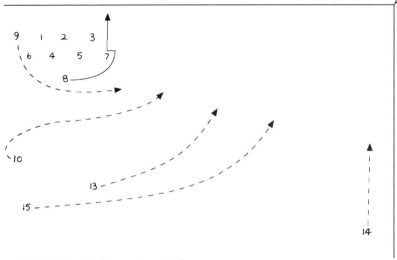

Fig. 61 **Distraction from a close attack**

- Why is it so important that 10, 13 and 15 run across initially?
- In particular what should they beware of in going forward?

Timing
- What balance of power in the packs is needed?
- When does the decision-maker announce the projected attack?
- When does he give the first 'go' signal?
- When does he give the second 'go' signal?
  (a) In relation to his team?
  (b) In relation to their team?
- In what sequence do 10, 13, 15 and 14 set off?
- Is it better for 14 to go just too early or just too late?
- If 4(a) and 4(b) aren't in effective accord, what can the coach alter?
- When can the backs happily switch from going across to going forward?

Decision-making
- Positive answers to which questions above indicate the attack?
- Who is best placed to co-ordinate/call the attack?
- At what point must the final option on attacks – forward or back – be exercised?
- What factors shape that choice?

- If the attack is forward, and the opposition check it, what areas might 9 and 10 be thinking of attacking in second phase?
- It's the last minute, and we're losing by five points: to what extent does this affect our thinking about opting for the forward or the back attack?

The answers I'd give to these questions are implicit in what I've written, but it's not particularly important that we should agree on answers. At the back of our minds are different teams, different traditions, that shape us towards particular answers. It is important that we try to clarify, understand, and develop the mental process that helps us set up attacks of this kind effectively.

THE PEEL FROM THE LINE-OUT

A typical case in which the coach's ability to organise the interaction of space and time, his inventiveness, and ability to refine techniques, combine to give good results is with the 'peel' from the line-out.

It's a promising situation to concentrate on: if we can take the ball a metre forward, we've crossed the gain-line and the forward defence line. If we can take it wide of the opposing forwards, we can expect to go at least 5m, and outflank the opposing pack, before we meet opposition. If we are checked there, we'll have an interesting split-field situation to exploit which looks as if it can easily be developed. It's evidently going to be one way of pressurising a drift defence against our backs. Moreover, we've all seen that it can work spectacularly well. So how can we make it a little more effective for our own team?

We can start by sorting out the factors involved, and looking for higher efficiency in each.

1. The throw

This is the single most important factor. If the throw isn't accurate, it's impossible to organise any aspect of line-out play to an acceptable level. It's a good case of technical coaching, which we can summarise as:

- you find and use your best thrower – who may or may not be your hooker;
- it's helpful to use a forward – it minimises disruption of practices and allows specialisation;
- you offer a simple mechanical model of throwing:
  (a) weight shift from back to front, but always in balance;
  (b) check no blocking by front hip;
  (c) hips lead shoulders for as long as possible;
  (d) chest up as long as possible;
  (e) elbow leads arm movement;

(f) hand up the desired line of flight;

(g) chin up;

- you advise on the need for concentration:

  (a) think only of the throw;

  (b) visualise the flight of the ball;

- you emphasise the need for practice and self-coaching;

  (a) feedback from jumper every time;

  (b) feedback from mark you throw at in practice;

  (c) cause from effect: check through probable faults with him.

2. The length of throw

The longer the throw the greater the exaggeration of error, and the greater the effect of extraneous factors. In deciding to employ the long throw you have to assess the probability of success, and weigh it against the advantages. It obviously pays to throw not to the back man but to one from the back:

- the last man is useful as tidier up, and to prevent opponents straying offside;

- this lets the jumper concentrate on jumping;

- it gives the ball-receiver a little extra cover, behind which he can concentrate undisturbed by opposition pressure, and where defence of a mistake is easier.

3. The jumper

If we have a marked advantage in height or lifting power at the end of the line-out, it's an obvious indication, other things being equal, that we should try the peel. It's very much a matter of physical advantage, though: it's difficult to obtain an advantage by surprise or speed.

If we don't have such an advantage we can move either one or both of our regular jumpers to the back for the occasion. It's usual to accompany this move by putting a possible jumper at 2 – someone capable of doing a timed jump, if he is left unattended. But the shift of jumpers to the back will also help to bring our best runners/handlers to the front – which is an advantage in the peel.

4. Speed

It's surprising how often the opposition will not follow the shifted jumpers. But you can limit their thinking time by arranging that the shift and the throw should occur simultaneously. What we want is a clear call for the changed formation as we approach the line. You can set up intensive practice of this by simply having alternate throws in practice on the centre and 10m lines, calling each time. You can also build it into team practice by playing line-out and play from a line-out as an unopposed theme: put a ball on each line up the pitch (or arrange for the spare ball to appear on the next line!); play each one through second phase; and dash back to the next ball.

5. Aim of the jumper

If you can define this precisely, you'll simplify this job. He wants to drop the ball, slowly, close to the line of touch, slightly in front of his own position.

If it drops fast, it makes the timing of the run much more critical.

If it goes deep, it means the runner has to go back for it, and gives the defender longer to get to him. And if he misses it, it's much harder to defend.

If it goes behind the jumper, it means that the runner has to contend not only with catching the ball, but with simultaneous pressure from the opposition. Anyone at the end of the line is well advised to keep the ball in front of them, where the line gives protection, especially on the opposition throw.

The best advice to the jumper is to commit himself to the ball, with relaxed, spread fingers at right-angles to the ball's flight – always play down the line – and then gently push it slightly out and down. It's got to have the gentleness of real strength, which means getting the active shoulder up high.

6. Aim of jump supporters

The aim of 4, 5, 6, and 7 in the line-out – who will not necessarily be the players wearing those numbers – is simple: lift, or compress and apply pressure. These are the aims of all players in the line-out at all times. When the ball comes down we want:

- to have a tight wall in that area – those in front of the catcher move back towards him, and those behind move forward; and
- to be as nearly as possible directly under the ball when it comes down.

The degree to which they can apply these simple aims depends of the views of the referee. As is so often the case, it's his interpretation of the law that's important. If he says we can't do it, we get as close to it as he'll allow; if he won't allow it at all, we won't do it at all.

You'll also note that the jumper himself is aiming to take off as close to the midline as the referee and the opposition will allow. He needs as much horizontal movement as possible to create energy for the lift. The keynote is concentration on action: nobody simply ball-watches.

7. Ball-receivers

The alteration in our line-up should work to our advantage if it lets us have good handlers and good runners catching the ball. We needn't, however, assume that these will appear in particular positions: it's probable they will, but by no means certain.

Now let's review the situation. If all has gone well, we've got the ball dropping slowly, near but not at the tail of the line, near the line of touch. This in itself is very useful, for example for setting up a maul. But we want to use it to launch an attack by the forwards. For that attack to work we need the following:

(i) Running speed

We've all seen the receiver running fast down the line, and having to check because the ball hasn't arrived. That check kills the start. We've seen the receiver running, and not making it: the ball's gone down. But the first mistake is far more common. It means that there has been no control over the timing. If the player starts early over a limited distance it's evident that he'll either have to run slow, or slow down – neither of much utility. It is virtually always the case that the player is starting too early: he has to check for a moment before starting his run. The exact timing is determined by trial and error in practice, and established by intensive repetition. This will lead to a physical state in the receiver akin to what he'll experience in the match, and will help to establish the working range within which the operation will be successful.

The second determinant of the speed at which he can run on to the ball is the space available for acceleration. It's at best limited, and this suggests that he should start from the front of the line-out.

(ii) Immediate support

Even if we now have our receiver running fast on to the ball, we still face the problem of getting him past the end of the line. We can arrange for our tail man to give him cover, but it's very hard to effect. We must expect him to be under pressure as he approaches the end of the line. What we need is support available immediately it's needed. It's no good if it's a metre behind: he's got to be able to hand the ball on, if necessary, almost at the moment he receives it. For this we want the supporter running virtually alongside him, shielded by him from the opposition. This will also give us a little more cover if the deflection is too hard or too deep.

This player has to be running at the same speed as the receiver, but he has to get outside him. The way to do this is obvious, once you see it. I saw it because a player did it. Our No. 2 had been trying to catch our No. 1 and was quite unable to do so. I didn't want to slow 1 down. Then instead of waiting for 1 to pass him, 2 moved first, turning and getting behind 1's line of run. He then accelerated alongside the receiver in perfect position to cover the deflection and take the pass.

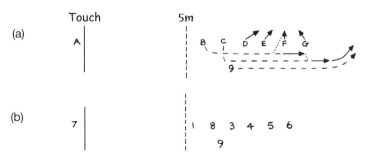

Fig. 62 Setting up the peel

8. Getting the overload

We've taken the first step towards the required overload in getting the first supporter alongside. We can add to it if the scrum-half has been briefed to see himself as the ultimate fast striker. One advantage of incorporating him is that he can move along deeper than 1 and 2, to give more cover against mistakes, and that running from deeper he should get a better angle in attack. You need to experiment with the depth and the timing to get him into an effective position.

But even given two supporters, we have to guard against the check when we meet the opposing stand-off and centre. To get that far and lose possession is a waste of energy and position. So we need to drill into every member of the pack that it's a combined operation, and that we want every forward driving over the tackle ball, and getting beyond it. But this is not to be done at the expense of their first job: contributing to our getting that ball. As soon as the first job is well and truly done, everyone merging under the ball, and the deflection safely in hand, then the entire pack leaves for the possible ruck.

So there are two main stages in coaching: the technical setting up of the mechanical side, so that everyone knows exactly what his role is; and the repetition practice ending every time in the contact situation. Occasionally we may get the ball away to our support. If not, we're dropping our shoulder and driving forward, with the ball left behind.

9. Angle of run

A further decision needs to be made about angle of run by the ball-carrier. How soon does he start to drive upfield? The problem is that to change direction fast inevitably slows him down; to change direction immediately after passing the end of the line brings him into contact with their forward cover. Both of these options are limiting, unless our ball-carrier is physically better adapted to contact than to running. There's a lot to be said for getting clear on a flattish run, before sweeping forward. It does make it a little harder to support, but that, for me, is outweighed by the need to go forward.

10. Alternatives

We need to build in, and work on, alternatives. If every time we change our line or throw long we're doing a peel, well, the opposition may not be bright, but they aren't blind. And we need to cover in case things go wrong. What can we do?

First, when we switch positions, we put a possible jumper at 2. He may be our No. 8, who will certainly be useful both as jumper and as support runner. However, it's a slight help if he doesn't look like a jumper, and doesn't attract attention. He dummies the peel start, and immediately goes into a timed jump. For this he needs to be coached just as you'd coach your jumpers, and supporters.

I'd like to suggest, however, as particularly applicable here and generally applicable to front jumpers, that the coach look very carefully at an alternative jumping method. This allows a very efficient use of available power, and is extremely fast in operation. Its central feature is a reversal of feet – the outside foot is forward. It's evidently best to take off from the inside foot and the method allows:

- a long, fast, flat take-off strike instead of a shuffle;
- getting the inside foot as close to the centre line as the referee will allow;
- getting that inside foot in front of the opponent so that you get up before he does; and
- a disguised take-off, since the player actually benefits from turning to face his opponent exactly as he might do if he intended to set off for the back peel.

This is the foundation of the best – centimetre-for-centimetre – jumping I've ever seen. It also ties in beautifully in its speed and height with the timed throw. I'd thoroughly recommend that your jumper experiments with it.

From this position, we can – provided we're within a metre or so of the opposing line – attack round the front. The runner for this ball needs power and determination rather than speed – in fact speed might be a disadvantage to him, making him easier to push into touch. To expect him to go forward more than a metre, even with the thrower trying to force him back in, is unrealistic.

Second, a normal deflection to the scrum-half from our substitute jumper gives us the chance of running the ball with their back row several yards worse off than usual relative to our stand-off.

Third, we can throw long but to the nearer of our jumpers, to push down in the middle of our line. This gives a good chance of setting up a driving maul with considerable freedom in how we use the ball.

11. Second-phase preparations/intensive practice

The peel is a typical unopposed theme. You can work your way right down the field, with the ball not in use waiting for you at the next line, You call for the changed line as you approach, and go straight into it. You play the peel, and arrange a maul or ruck, from which the TDM calls an attack to use the available space, and the possible absence of an opposing back under the maul. As soon as the run is executed and the ball brought back in from the wing – to ensure constant support – we go on to the next line.

Once it's established, the coach can build it into any other team practice he's running.

THE FORWARDS FEED THE BACKS AND
THE BACKS FEED THE FORWARDS

Much of the previous section focused on forwards initiating their own attacks from tactical points. Typically, they're launched from the optimum position – very close to the gain-line. But they suffer in terms of a limited acceleration zone, limited choice of direction, and lack of immediately available space. These problems diminish if we can arrange for the backs to hand the ball back to the forwards in a planned situation. To get this happening effectively, we need first to convince the backs that it's in their interest. There's no better way of exposing the weaknesses of a drift defence, and there's no better ball than that from a quick heel after a forward attack. In the integrated team, the forwards feed the backs and the backs feed the forwards.

It's true that your backs already supply ball to supporting forwards, but:

- the forwards may have to go back for it, and successful attack is unlikely;
- the ball becomes available wide, where the forwards' angle of run tends to be across rather than forward; and
- the ball is made available when conditions have already deteriorated – after a tackle, or while the back is being held and the area is already strewn with bodies.

The aim of consciously feeding the forwards is to do so with attacking conditions in their favour. So we can say:

- the forwards will have time to reach a position from which they can accelerate forward on to the ball;
- the hand-over point will be close to the tactical point rather than wide; and
- the hand-over takes place while the back is still free to choose his action.

So we have to set up such situations, work out the necessary limits in time and space within which they'll work, practise until they are slick, and incorporate them in our unopposed.

The key idea is that of the double switch. The backs set themselves up for an attack wide, but work a switch so that the ball is brought back towards the tactical point; the forwards use this time to drop back and wide. The forwards then accelerate on their chosen line, to execute the second switch with the back, and take the ball forward and out. Often, the first to handle will be the honorary fourth man in the back row – your scrum-half, who has that much more time to get into position.

Look at Fig 63. You'll see that fly-half and inside-centre have set off across field, with the fullback and the wing motoring up wide as the intended strike force. This is a real possibility: I've seen beautiful tries scored off this start. The flat-running fly-half is very difficult for the opposing open-side flanker to ignore: he'll tend to chase him. This creates a little more time for outside-centre to carry the ball back. There's a real possibility of him continuing his run, swinging out into space. But he'll certainly absorb the attention of the later-breaking opposition forwards.

While this is going on, our strikers have dropped back – to create an acceleration zone – and wide – so that they can cut down the distance the outside-centre has to carry the ball. What they'd like would be for the outside-centre to have enough space to give the ball not to the first supporter, but to the second. This means that the striking ball-carrier will have support inside him and out. (This simple but effective idea should be in the mind of wingers feeding inside supporters – get it two inside – or wingers in sevens cutting inside and getting a couple of players outside them before switching the ball. Or, better still, turning to run with the two outside supporters.)

When you're setting this up, you need to explain clearly what the intention is and the basic mechanism by which we intend to carry it out. Let the players get inside it; walk through, so that they feel what it's going to be like. Make sure that they are happy with it, and that it's going to work for them. Is the outside-centre fast enough to carry the ball, and tough enough to risk running at the opposing pack? Would your team be better doing it from inside centre? As you walk through, you'll start to get a sense of the parameters: how far apart the front three can afford to stand; how late the centre can change direction; how far you can realistically expect him to carry the ball; how deep the strike force can get; which of them is best placed/qualified to be the striker; and so on. This process is one of the most pleasing in coaching. The coach and players can *make* it work – indeed, they've *got* to make it work: if they don't answer all the questions realistically, it'll be embarrassing in the extreme. Recognise the fact: the parameters will be different for each set of players. There's no single right answer.

Once you've got it going, and feel happy with it in the harsh testing ground of the match, ask yourself: 'Can we use this mechanism in another situation?' You need to ask this of every start that you employ: if it works for you in situation A, you can probably transfer it to situation B. For example, you've a scrum, your put-in, 20m away from the right touch. How about your No. 8 passing directly to your winger once your 9 and 7 have had time to drop out and take the switch ball from 14 cutting back? 14 runs to pull in the opposing winger as well as their back row, and hopes to release the two-man strike force up the touch-line. Handle it the same way: walk through it, discuss what factors will affect it – for example, against what teams can you afford to let 7 drop back before the ball is released? You may not be able to do it against every team, but it might win the game against the right teams. Once again, you'll enjoy shaping it to fit your particular players.

The double switch is a start I like because it works well. But experiment. For example, from a line-out, have your fly-half run for the tail of the line, with your scrum-half or a back row forward dropping back ready for the switch. As the opposing end man puts pressure on, the fly-half curves back in slightly as if he's being forced to do it; this pulls the end man across and opens the way for the switch strike.

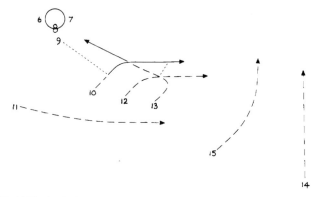

Fig 63 The backs bring the ball back to the forwards

This is an open-ended start, full of attacking possibilities. We're never locked in till the final choice of strike. It's excellent for launching the back row into space behind the opposing back row.

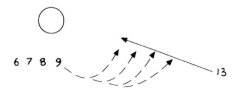

Fig 64 The forwards drop back and wide

The time 10 takes to run the ball wide, and 13 takes to bring it back, makes it easy for 6, 7, 8 and 9 to get back into a support position from which they can accelerate on to the ball.

(a)   (b)

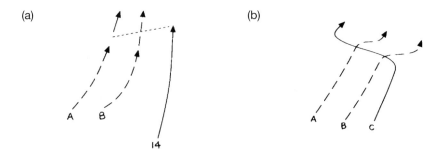

Fig. 65 13, if he's under pressure, can give the ball to the first man he passes

However, he creates a better attacking opportunity if he gives the ball to the second, third or fourth player

(a) The winger with support inside him.

(b) The winger cutting back (for example in sevens). C dummies to B and A, then cuts back out as part of a three-man attack.

Index